ACTS OF THE XIX PROVINCIAL CHAPTER

AND

CUMULATIVE STATUTES

OF THE

PROVINCE OF SAINT ALBERT THE GREAT, U.S.A.

JUNE 11, 2015 – JUNE 24, 2015

SAINT DOMINIC PRIORY

SAINT LOUIS, MISSOURI

MISSION STATEMENT

The Dominican Friars
of the Province of St. Albert the Great
communicate the Word of God through
preaching,
theological education
and the promotion of justice and peace.

This mission in the Body of Christ
demands vowed community life, liturgical prayer
and life-long study. [99/35]

Contents

ACTS OF THE 2015 PROVINCIAL CHAPTER

APPENDICES

PRELIMINARY NOTES

1. LCO: Throughout these pages, the citation LCO refers to *Liber Constitutionum et Ordinationum*, published by the General Chapter of River Forest in 1968, and modified by subsequent General Chapters.

2. ACTS: Throughout these pages, the citation ACTS refers to ACTS of previous provincial chapters preceded by an identifying numerical calendar reference. The STATUTES refer to the Cumulative Statutes which appear in Appendix A of the Acts.

3. STATUTE: An ordinance, quasi-permanent in nature, which regulates the life and government of communities and a province. It begins to bind with the promulgation of the Acts of a provincial chapter and retains its force until revoked, modified, or otherwise changed by another provincial chapter (LCO 279, 286, I).

4. ORDINATION: A norm or regulation, transitory in nature, which concerns the life and government of communities and a province. It begins to bind with the promulgation of the Acts of a provincial chapter and remains in force only until the promulgation of the Acts of the following provincial chapter, at which time it lapses if not renewed (LCO 286, II).

5. RECOMMENDATIONS: A statement of suggestion, encouragement, or direction: reminders given by a provincial chapter concerning aspects of the life and government of a province.

6. COMMISSION: A directive given by a provincial chapter to an individual brother or to a specific group to accomplish a certain task.

7. DECLARATION: A statement in which a chapter calls the

attention of the brethren to certain practices and policies, or clarifies and interprets provincial legislation.

8. PETITION: A request made by a provincial chapter to the Master of the Order or to a General Chapter in matters which exceed the competence of a provincial chapter.

9. APPOINTMENT: A designation of a brother for an office or position, or to membership on standing or temporary committees established by a provincial chapter. Appointment may also be committed to the Provincial – alone or with the Council – for decision. Appointments to an office or standing committee perdure until successors are appointed, ordinarily by a provincial chapter or by the Provincial and the Council.

10. COMMENDATION: An expression of gratitude or approbation given by a provincial chapter to individuals or groups.

Fratres Ordinis Praedicatorum
CURIA GENERALITIA

Rome, July 22, 2015

*fr. James Marchionda and the brothers of the
Province of St. Albert the Great, U.S.A.*

Prol. 35/15/540 CP

Dear brother James,

Having read attentively the Acts of your Nineteenth Provincial Chapter celebrated in the Priory of St. Dominic, in St. Louis, Missouri, U.S.A. from 11 June - 24 June, 2015, and having consulted with members of the General Council, I hereby approve the Acts and the changes made to the Statutes of the Province.

In light of the Jubilee of the Order, your concise Acts emphasize a renewal in evangelization that stems from an honest evaluation of the fraternal and apostolic life in the province. This includes an evaluation of your current provincial commitments, the way in which you engage each other in the fraternal life, an emphasis on permanent formation, and a reminder of the call to mendicancy. Also, you have the foresight to give to new leaders the necessary leadership training that they will need for ministry with all of its complexities.

The need for an evaluation of all of your provincial missions in a process of planning and priorities, which was highlighted in my letter to you after your recent canonical visit, is necessary. This process is a coming together of the local community projects and the provincial project as a whole. The synergy between them is a dynamic time of renewal. However, there does not seem to be a strong emphasis on a process, as presented in your Acts, to include explicitly a consultation that is province-wide or at least at provincial assemblies. From the Acts it could be understood that the process is the responsibility solely of the prior provincial and his council. Perhaps, in trying to be concise in the Acts, certain assumptions were made. In approving these Acts, I have asked that before their promulgation, amendments be made to make explicit that the process of planning and priorities is to be accomplished through a serious consultation of the entire province.

As I recall from my recent canonical visit with you, the Dominican Family is an important part of your collaboration in mission. However, there was little about this in your Acts. I hope that as you look to your process of planning and priorities that you will draw upon the wealth of the collaboration within the Dominican Family, which you have fostered over the years.

At this point I would like to thank you for your generosity in the foreign missions, especially in your development and support of the new Vice-Province in Bolivia. Your recommendation to continue to explore a new foreign mission with a stable community is commendable. I look forward to being a part of your reflection on this possible new venture.

Permanent formation is very much underlined in the Acts. It is a key part of our continued growth in maturity and the spiriual life. In keeping with the General Chapter of Trogir, though it is not well cited in your Acts. highlighting the importance of faith sharing in communities is to be commended. As each conmunity plans its days of permanent formation, I also ask that you think about reflecting on a spirituality of aging, which I have asked several provinces to consider. I note with interest your challenge to societal behaviors that give greater importance to texting than to being present to those you are with.

Mendicancy is an essential part of our life. Your Acts underline its importance for the sake of the mission of the province as well as for the formation and for the healthcare of the brothers. At the same time, you are concerned about others and the call to share what you can through a solidarity fund. For all of this to become stronger, it is fundamental to base it on sound accounting practices, and proper benchmarks for evaluation as you have noted. My visitation letter underlined the importance of balanced budgets and addressing fiscal deficits.

Regarding economy, the Acts do not make explicit the spending limits at the provincial and local level. Therefore, I have asked that the limits in the 2011 Provincial Acts be incorporated into these Acts before their promulgation.

One of the major concerns during the canonical visit was the province's mission at Aquinas Institute. I appreciate that you have taken into account in your deliberations the comments that I made regarding a Moderator of Studies and an Academic Advisor for Dominican Students (the latter position now being abolished). At the same time, considering how important this topic was for your province, I am disappointed that Aquinas Institute, School of Theology, was not treated in a more profound manner. Perhaps, this is not possible at a provincial chapter. However, the statennent of 'reaffirmation' does not take into account the complexity of the decision that the province needs to make for the future of the academic formation of its brothers. A more comprehensiive process is necessary, like the one outlined in my visitation letter to you. Therefore, I ask the prior provincial and his council, especially in their role as Members of the Corporation of Aquinas Institute, to implement such a process that will result in the clarification of what it means corncretely, as noted in your Acts, that "the primary purpose of Aquinas Institute is the education of Dominican brothers." What does this mean for the academic formation of new generations of Dominican brothers in our intellectual tradition. Furthermore, the important discussions to take place in the communities of the province should be done after the brothers receive the necessarry data for their conversations. Too often we meet without being well informed. This results in making decisions based on past and current assumptions. Our dedication to study ought to keep us from this common hazard.

Before concluding, I would like to thank fr. Charles Bouchard for his fraternal leadership and ministry to all of you during his term as prior provincial. I also assure fr. James Marchionda of my prayers during these years of service as your prior provincial. Also, I am grateful for the dedicated service of' fr. Michael Mascari as Socius for Intellectual Life at the General Curia. Furthermore, I wish to thank you and our brothers for their ministry at the Angelicum during this important time of transition: frs. Dominic Holz, Michael Monshau, and Albert Glade who now has moved to the Convittto.

I remain grateful to all of you for your witness to the renewal in our Dominican life and mission during these Jubilee years. Be assured of my prayers for all of you.

Your brother in St. Dominic,

fr. Franklin Buitrago Rojas, O.P.
a secretis

fr. Bruno Cadoré, O.P.
Master of the Order

FORMALITIES

1. The XIX Provincial Chapter of the Province of Saint Albert the Great, U.S.A., was convoked by the Prior Provincial, Charles Bouchard, O.P., on 25 September 2014.

2. The XIX Provincial Chapter of the Province of Saint Albert the Great, U.S.A., convened on June 11, 2015 at Saint Dominic Priory in Saint Louis, Missouri. Leobardo Almazán, O.P., Vicar of the Province, was the chairman of the Chapter.

    The Mass of the Holy Spirit was held on the same day the Chapter convened. At this Mass the following (18) brothers who had died since the last Provincial Chapter were remembered:

    Edward L. Cleary, O.P.
    Kevin D. O'Rourke, O.P.
    John R. Dolehide, O.P.
    Benedict G. Baer, O.P.
    Joseph P. Kenny, O.P.
    Benedict M. Ashley, O.P.
    Roderick M. Brown, O.P.
    Jerome M. Walsh, O.P.
    John H. Gerlach, O.P.
    Michael G. Kyte, O.P.
    Thomas A. Morrison, O.P.
    Gilbert L. Hensely, O.P.
    Wilfred Gabriel F. Hoff, O.P.
    Bede R. Jagoe, O.P.
    Benjamin J. Russell, O.P.
    Robert J. Botthof, O.P.
    John C. Fabian, O.P.
    Frank M. Nouza, O.P.

3. The following vocals were convened for the Provincial Chapter:

Priors

Louis S. Morrone, O.P., Priory of Saint Pius V, Chicago, Illinois

Simon-Felix Michalski, O.P., Priory of Blessed Sacrament, Madison, Wisconsin

James Spahn, O.P., Priory of Saint Albert the Great, Minneapolis, Minnesota

Matthew Strabala, O.P., Priory of Saint Vincent Ferrer, River Forest, Illinois

David Wright, O.P., Priory of Saint Dominic, Denver, Colorado

Leobardo Almazán, O.P., Priory of Saint Dominic, Saint Louis, Missouri

Socii

James Marchionda, O.P., Priory of Saint Pius V, Chicago, Illinois

Thomas Lynch, O.P., Priory of Saint Pius V, Chicago, Illinois

DePorres Durham, O.P., Priory of Blessed Sacrament, Madison, Wisconsin

Herbert Hayek, O.P., Priory of Saint Albert the Great, Minneapolis, Minnesota

Thomas McDermott, O.P., Priory of Saint Vincent Ferrer, River Forest, Illinois

Luke Barder, O.P., Priory of Saint Dominic, Denver, Colorado

Paul Whittington, O.P., Priory of Saint Dominic, Saint Louis, Missouri

Delegates of the Colleges

Jay Harrington, O.P, of the First Electoral College

Paul Byrd, O.P., of the Second Electoral College

Richard Litzau, O.P., of the Third Electoral College

Jude McPeak, O.P., of the Fourth Electoral College

Past Prior Provincial

Charles Bouchard, O.P.

4. According to *LCO* 358, § I, 1, the three senior vocals of the chapter were named as examiners: David Wright, O.P., James

Marchionda, O.P., and Herbert Hayek, O.P. The examiners reviewed and approved the testimonial letters for the *socii* and the delegates. There being no challenges, the examiners approved all of the vocals.

5. With the consent of the vocals, the Vicar approved Kevin Niehoff, O.P., as secretary, and Raymond Bryce, O.P., Samuel Hakeem, O.P., and James Peter Trares, O.P., as assistant secretaries (*LCO* 358, § I, 2).

6. The vocals approved four commissions (*LCO*, § I, 3):

Evangelization:
    James Spahn, O.P. – Chairman
    Paul Byrd, O.P.
    Vincent Davila, O.P.
    Thomas Lynch, O.P.
    James Marchionda, O.P.
    Simon-Felix Michalski, O.P.

Intellectual Life:
    David Wright, O.P. – Chairman
    Leobardo Almazán, O.P.
    Jay Harrington, O.P.
    Thomas McDermott, O.P.
    Matthew Strabala, O.P.

Leadership:
    Jude McPeak, O.P. – Chairman
    DePorres Durham, O.P.
    Louis Morrone, O.P.
    Paul Whittington, O.P.

Mendicancy:
    Luke Barder, O.P., – Chairman
    Charles Bouchard, O.P.
    Herbert Hayek, O.P.

Richard Litzau, O.P.

7. On June 17, 2015, the process for the election of the Prior Provincial began. Following the norms of *LCO* 448, § IV, the vocals elected Paul Byrd, O.P., first teller, and Jude McPeak, O.P., second teller.

Following the norms of *LCO* 451 – 452, 502 – 508, James V. Marchionda, O.P., was elected Prior Provincial of the Province of Saint Albert the Great, U.S.A. The election was approved by Bruno Cadoré, O.P., Master of the Order (see Prot. No. 35/15/465 CP, June 18, 2015).

James Marchionda, O.P., accepted his office (*LCO* n. 470, § I), and assumed his office with the required public profession of faith on June 18, 2015 at 8:30 a.m. at the conclusion of Mass in the chapel at St. Dominic Priory, Saint Louis, Missouri (*LCO* n. 471).

8. The vocals determined to elect four diffinitors consecu-tively, and elected the following brothers (*LCO* n. 515):

Leobardo Almazán, O.P.
David Wright, O.P.
Paul Byrd, O.P.
Kevin Niehoff, O.P.

The vocals also elected three provincial councilors and two alternate provincial councilors (*LCO* 519, § I; Provincial Statute 44, IV).

Thomas O'Meara, O.P., First Councilor
James Spahn, O.P., Second Councilor
Simon-Felix Michalski, O.P., Third Councilor

Thomas Jackson, O.P., First Alternate Councilor
Matthew Strabala, O.P., Second Alternate Councilor

9. The following friars were elected to their respective offices for general chapters:

Richard Peddicord, O.P., Diffinitor, First General Chapter
Thomas McDermott, O.P., Socius, First General Chapter
Andrew-Carl Wisdom, O.P., Diffinitor, Second General Chapter
Jay Harrington, O.P., Socius, Second General Chapter
Charles Bouchard, O.P., Socius to the Provincial for a General Chapter

10. The diffinitorium made the following assignments:
The Diffinitorium decided to present Jay Harrington, O.P., to the Master of the Order for appointment as Regent of Studies.

Socius to the Provincial and Vicar Provincial
                                                Louis Morrone, O.P.
Syndic of the Province   Kevin Niehoff, O.P.
Provincial Archivist   Louis Morrone, O.P.
Assistant Provincial Archivist   David Wright, O.P.
Promoter of Vocations   Andrew McAlpin, O.P.
Promoter of Social Justice   Brendan Curran, O.P.
Promoter of Causes   Paul Byrd, O.P.
Promoter of the Holy Name Confraternity
                                                Nicholas Monco, O.P.
Promoter of the Holy Rosary Confraternity
                                                Michail Ford, O.P.
Representative to the Dominican Volunteers, U.S.A.
                                                Simon-Felix Michalski, O.P.
Representative to the Priestly Fraternities
                                                Thomas McDermott, O.P.
Promoter of Preaching   Gregory Heille, O.P.
Promoter of the Angelic Warfare   Andrew McAlpin, O.P.
Promoter of Permanent Formation   Paul Whittington, O.P.
Promoter of the Dominican Laity   Seve Kuhlmann, O.P.
Promoter of the Dominican Family   Luke Barder, O.P.
Director of the New Priory Press   Andrew McAlpin, O.P.

11. The Diffinitorium made the following appointments to the various councils and commissions (terms end on August 31st of the year indicated, unless otherwise noted):

Admissions Board

Andrew McAlpin, O.P., Chair	*ex officio*
James Marchionda, O.P.	*ex officio*
Daniel Davis, O.P.	2016
Edward van Merrienboer, O.P.	2017
Kevin Stephens, O.P.	2018
Thomas Jackson, O.P.	2018
Simon-Felix Michalski, O.P.	2019
Jude McPeak, O.P.	2019

Provincial Formation Council (all terms *ex officio*)
Louis Morrone, O.P. (Prior Provincial's delegate)
Jay Harrington, O.P. (Regent of Studies)
Paul Whittington, O.P. (Promoter of Permanent Formation)
Andrew McAlpin, O.P. (Promoter of Vocations)
Members of the Local Formation Councils of Denver and St. Louis
A Student Representative

Intellectual Life Commission

Jay Harrington, O.P., Chair	*ex officio*
Paul Whittington, O.P.	*ex officio*
Robert Keller, O.P.	2016
Kevin Stephens, O.P.	2017
Richard Peddicord, O.P.	2018
Harry Byrne, O.P.	2019

Board of Examiners of Ordinandi

Leo Almazán, O.P.	Harry Byrne, O.P.
Gregory Heille, O.P.	Dominic McManus, O.P.

David Delich, O.P.   Donald Goergen, O.P.
Paul Philibert, O.P.   Kevin Stephens, O.P.
De Porres Durham, O.P.   Jay Harrington, O.P.
Thomas Poulsen, O.P.

Economic Council
  Kevin Niehoff, O.P., Provincial Syndic   *ex officio*
  Andrew Carl Wisdom, O.P., Vicar for OMA   *ex officio*
  Louis S. Morrone, O.P   2017
  De Porres Durham, O.P.   2019
  Mr. Kevin Hanley   until August 31, 2017
  Mr. Ben Jagoe   until August 31, 2018
  Mrs. Jean Finnegan   until August 31, 2019

Commission on Social Justice
  Brendan Curran, O.P., Chair   *ex officio*
  Joseph Minuth, O.P.   2016
  Douglas-Adam Greer, O.P.   2017
  Lorenzo Laorden, O.P.   2018
  Thomas Lynch, O.P.   2019

Committee of the Retirement Plan
  James V. Marchionda, O.P.   *ex officio*
  Kevin Niehoff, O.P.   *ex officio*
  Michael Winkels, O.P.   2017
  Patrick Norris, O.P.   2018
  Ed Riley, O.P.   2019

12.   The Diffinitorium made the following decisions and pastoral appointments.

James Spahn, O.P., Pastor of Holy Rosary-Santo Rosario Parish, Minneapolis, Minnesota, shall be proposed to the diocesan bishop for a term renewal of three years.

José Santiago, O.P., shall be presented to the Archbishop of Chicago for appointment as Pastor of St. Pius V Parish,

17

Chicago, Illinois, for a six-year term, to be effective August 1, 2015.

Joseph P. Gillespie, O.P., Pastor of St. Albert the Great Parish, Minneapolis, Minnesota, shall be proposed to the diocesan bishop for a term renewal of three years.

In accord with LCO 264, St. Thomas Aquinas Priory in Albuquerque, New Mexico, shall be reduced from the status of a convent to that of a house.

PETITION: The XIX Provincial Chapter petitions the Master of the Order to suppress the Convent of St. Thomas Aquinas in River Forest, Illinois.

13. The Diffinitorium, in accord with the current *Ratio Formationis Particularis* of the Province, made the following appointments for the Local Formation Councils in Denver, Colorado (Novitiate) and St. Louis, Missouri (Studentate):

Formation Council – Denver, Colorado:
Robert Keller, O.P., Master of Novices, Chair
David Wright, O.P., Prior
Edward Ruane, O.P.

Formation Council – St. Louis, Missouri:
Donald Goergen, O.P., Master of Students, Chair
Leobardo Almazán, O.P., Prior
Jay Harrington, O.P., Regent of Studies

EVANGELIZATION

14. Dominican evangelization is born of study and contemplation of the Word, brought into dialogue with the world. Intellectually rigorous, and founded in our Thomistic tradition, it seeks Truth and Good everywhere. It is hopeful and

positive, based on God's love for Creation. It sees the value of cultural expressions of faith and religion--even if different from those of the preacher--for God has often spoken through them long before we speak. Dominican evangelization is communal and collaborative, availing itself of all possible means to reach people's hearts. Dominican evangelization is itinerant, carrying the preacher to the margins and frontiers (be they socio-economic, intellectual, geographical, cultural, etc.) of where the Gospel is proclaimed. At the heart of this evangelization is the witness of our lives, which, as our primary preaching, demands an ever-deepening renewal of our regular life. Evangelization should be at the center of every Dominican ministry and community.

Dominican Evangelization And Focus

15. We COMMISSION that the Prior Provincial and his Council consider the concept of Dominican City Centers, as elaborated by the Commission on Evangelization, as they develop future assignments and ministerial commitments. (See Appendix.)

16. We ORDAIN that by 1 July 2017, the Prior Provincial and his Council in consultation with the province use a specialized assessment tool to perform a thorough assessment of all our ministries and the cities in which we minister so as to decide which ministries ought to be retained, which let go, and which new provincial projects might be begun based on the needs of the local and global Church. The process of assessment is to include a clear formulation of criteria for evaluation.

17. We RECOMMEND that this process utilize an accepted tool of assessment.

The Witness Of Our Common Life

18. We RECOMMEND that the superior and lector of local

communities lead a communal study of our Constitutions, specifically the Fundamental Constitutions and the First Distinction, Section One (*The Life of the Brothers: The Following of Christ*, LCO 2-153). This study should include reflection of how the local community can renew their living of these Constitutions in light of our 800th anniversary.

19.   We RECOMMEND that the superior and lector lead a study on Dominican spirituality, with a special focus on our historical roots (in an attempt to respond to Vatican II's call to return to our founding charism). Possible resources include (but are not limited to) Donald Goergen's *Letters to My Brothers and Sisters*, Paul Murray's *The New Wine of Dominican Spirituality: A Drink Called Happiness*, and Guy Bedouelle's *Saint Dominic: The Grace of the Word*.

20.   We COMMISSION the Promoter of Permanent Formation to devise a list of such resources and develop a syllabus for the study mentioned in (19, 20).

21.   We RECOMMEND that the Prior Provincial continue to offer pastoral reflections to the Province on questions surrounding our regular life.

22.   We EXHORT brothers to balance their ministerial commitments with their responsibility to the communal life, and to include their communal commitments in their schedules.

Prayer

23.   We EXHORT brothers to be mindful of LCO 58 and its call to make our prayer open to the public.

24.   We RECOMMEND that communities whose prayer is currently not open to the public have a discussion about how they might change their practice (e.g., location, time, etc.) to make their prayer more public.

25. We EXHORT the brothers to be mindful of LCO 66, §II, and its call for meditation.

26. We ORDAIN that each member and each community of the province pray regularly for vocations to the Order using the prayer developed for this purpose by the Provincial Chapter of 1999 (cf. Acts 1999, #64; Acts 2011, #33).

Community

27. We RECOMMEND that recreation be held daily in every community (cf. LCO 5), and COMMEND those communities who do so without television.

28. We RECOMMEND that local communities engage, at least monthly, in longer periods of communal recreation for the purpose of simply having fun together.

29. We EXHORT that brothers be mindful of their use of cell phones, etc., particularly in a communal setting, so that they may be more attentive to one another.

30. We RECOMMEND that local communities engage, at least monthly, in communal faith sharing in hopes of getting to know one another on a deeper level while experiencing themselves what it means to be a faith sharing community. Communities might consider setting aside an hour to reflect together on the readings for the coming Sunday and how they impact their lives (cf. *Evangelii Gaudium*, 153).

31. We COMMISSION the superior of each community to review every year the following forms of the brothers, (i.e. Power of Attorney, funeral arrangements, notice to next of kin, and Health Care Directives). These standardized forms are to be kept in the house and Provincial Office files (cf. Acts 2011, #39).

32.   We COMMISSION that superiors annually review driving qualifications for brothers over the age of seventy (cf. *Provincial Policy Handbook*, Driving Policy, page 63, e; Acts 2011, # 40).

33.   We COMMISSION the Provincial Formation Council to develop a workshop to assist senior members in formation communities to evaluate and assess novices and student brothers as the community discerns the readiness of these brothers for advancement in religious life. (Rome, 2010, #193-194, Bogota, 2007, #206-208, 216-217) (Acts 2011, #44).

Foreign Mission

34.   We ORDAIN that, before July 1, 2017, the Prior Provincial and his Council discuss taking on a foreign mission in consultation with the Master of the Order.

35.   We RECOMMEND that, should a mission be taken on, a sufficient number of friars be sent so that healthy com-munity life is possible.

800th Jubilee Celebration

36.   We COMMISSION local superiors with their communities to commit to specific ways they can publicly celebrate the Jubilee year (e.g., sponsoring a colloquium, concert of sacred music, lecture on Dominican history, participate together in a corporal work of mercy, etc.).

37.   We RECOMMEND the broad use of the following Jubilee Prayer of the Order in our communities and ministries:

> God, Father of mercy, who called your servant Dominic de Guzman to set out in faith as an itinerant pilgrim and a preacher of grace, as we prepare to

celebrate the Jubilee of the Order we ask you to pour again into us the Spirit of the Risen Christ, that we might faithfully and joyfully proclaim the Gospel of peace, through the same Jesus Christ our Lord. Amen

Dios Padre de misericordia, que llamaste a tu servidor Domingo de Guzmán a ponerse en camino en la fe, como peregrino itinerante y predicador de la gracia, al prepararnos a celebrar el Jubileo de la Orden, te pedimos que infundas de nuevo en nosotros el Espíritu de Cristo Resucitado, para que podamos proclamar con fidelidad y alegría el Evangelio de la paz, por Jesucristo nuestro Señor. Amén.

38.   We COMMISSION the Prior Provincial and his Council, in response to #65 of the Acta of the 2011 Chapter, to form an *ad hoc* commission to coordinate the provincial celebration of the 800th Jubilee. In addition, this commission should assist local communities *and* ministries in designing and imple-menting a plan for incorporating themes of the Jubilee into varied aspects of their lives (e.g., preaching, lecture series, bulletins, etc.).

39.   We RECOMMEND that the Communication and Marketing Department produce a pictorial directory of the Province to be published in 2016 and distributed to all friars of the Province.

Solidarity Fund For Dominican Home Missions

40.   We RECOMMEND that the prior provincial and the provincial council establish a solidarity fund for the Dominican home mission as called for by the 2011 provincial chapter (ACTS, #29-30).

41.   We COMMISSION that the Prior Provincial and his Council

establish a structure to manage this fund.

Communications And Internet Presence

42.   We RECOMMEND that each ministry designate a friar or layperson to maintain regular contact with and provide information to the Communication and Marketing Department of the Province.

MENDICANCY

43.   *"Voluntary poverty in this world enriches the soul and frees it from servitude. It makes us kind and meek, takes away our vain hope in transitory things, and gives us living faith and true hope"* (Catherine of Siena, Letter T206, to the Convent of Passignano of Valle Ombrosa).

"[Mendicancy] indicates a choice to live in dependence upon those to whom the preachers are sent, mirroring the dependence of Jesus and his disciples as they go through towns and villages proclaiming the Kingdom of God (Lk 8,1-3). [Bruno Cadore, 2014 Pastoral Letter on Mendicancy, 1; emphasis ours]

We EXHORT all members of the province to develop a "culture of mendicancy" at all levels of our life together.

Culture of Mendicancy

In the spirit of the Order's 800th Anniversary:

44.   We COMMISSION the Promoter of Permanent Formation, with the assistance of the Intellectual Life Commission, along with the Syndic of the province and in accord with LCO 251-ter. §I, to develop a syllabus on mendicancy that can be used in local communities. This syllabus should focus on spiritual

and theological formation on the three characteristics of mendicancy: poverty, dependence, and solidarity, in accord with the Master's *relatio* and 2014 Pastoral Letter on Mendicancy.

45. We COMMISSION conventual lectors to implement the syllabus on mendicancy in study meetings in their local communities.

46. We RECOMMEND that local communities explore ways to implement mendicancy in their common life, for example: The use of corporate credit cards, corporate cell phone plans, etc. Identifying and establishing relationships with local entities (i.e. the Knights of Columbus, other charitable organizations) with the view toward ongoing support for the mission, locally and provincially.

47. We RECALL to the attention of the brothers #28 of the Provincial Statutes (see also #29 of the 2011 Provincial Acta) which states:

    28. Our ministries often require resources beyond those available to the individual com-munity or the local community. We are to be willing to give support and approval to each other in our various ministries, provided that continuing evaluation gives evidence that they are meeting real pastoral needs. Local communities, as well as the Province, can support the ministries of individuals or of other com-munities by offering financial aid or housing facilities, and by encouraging brethren to join in these ministries. [73/58]

48. We COMMISSION the Prior Provincial and the Provincial Council to consider new practices and guidelines in how financial resources are shared among communities and ministries.

49. We RECOMMEND that the Prior Provincial invite Kathleen Hegenbart of Global Institutional Consulting to address the province at the next provincial assembly regarding the investments of the province.

Office for Mission Advancement

50. We COMMISSION the Prior Provincial and the Director of the Office for Mission Advancement to identify areas in our development efforts to be strengthened with particular concern for securing our long-term development needs.

51. We COMMISSION the Prior Provincial and the Director of the Office for Mission Advancement to further our development efforts by:
Promoting greater collaboration among provincial ministries with regard to our development efforts;
Providing formation in skills for development (i.e. fundraising, friendship development, asking, communication of mission identity, etc.);
Seeking effective participation in the 1216 Campaign (i.e. provide a script, create centralized list of possible donors, etc.).

52. We RECOMMEND that, when possible, the Prior Provincial and local superiors negotiate with the bishop in every diocese we serve to take up collections for the needs of the Province.

The Economic Council

53. We RECOMMEND that the Prior Provincial ensure that a member of the Economic Council has expertise in building projects and/or property management.

54. We RECOMMEND that the Economic Council convene more than twice a year.

55. We RECALL to the attention of the Prior Provincial and

Provincial Council their obligation to consult with the Economic Council as defined by LCO 581, II.

Reporting and Management

56. We RECALL the obligation for every community to produce and review a budget and discuss local finances at least once a year, per Provincial Statute 50.

57. We COMMISSION the Prior Provincial in consultation with the Provincial Council and Provincial Syndic to explore the need of hiring a Chief Financial Officer.

58. We COMMISSION the Prior Provincial and the Director of the Office for Mission Advancement with the Economic Council to evaluate our fundraising efforts against industry norms and Church standards in order to establish benchmarks to ensure ethical and efficient operation.

59. We COMMISSION the Prior Provincial and the Provincial Syndic to coordinate with local superiors and syndics in evaluating the extent of deferred maintenance on all provincial properties and develop a plan for addressing it. Moreover, deferred maintenance should be accounted as a liability on our balance sheets. A report is to be submitted by the Provincial Syndic to the Provincial Council by December 31, 2016.

60. We RECOMMEND that the Prior Provincial and the Provincial Council create an *ad hoc* committee to evaluate all our property holdings so as to recommend how best to utilize these assets. Before any action is taken on the recommendation, they would be reviewed by the Economic Council.

61. We RECOMMEND that the Prior Provincial and the Provincial Syndic meet with the Center for Priority Based Budgeting (CPBB) to consider undertaking a process that evaluates how

our resources are being allocated.

62.	We RECALL to the attention of the brothers #49a of the 2011 Provincial Acta which increased Provincial taxes to 25% for eight years, making allowances for houses and individual brothers that were unable to afford it and we ORDAIN that it shall remain in force for the foreseeable future, even until the next Provincial Chapter, with the additional revenues designated solely to retire the debt of Saint Dominic Priory in Saint Louis, Missouri.

63.	We ORDAIN that the annual Provincial budget approved by the Prior Provincial with his Council shall be the spending guide for the Provincial. The Provincial may spend or grant permission to spend up to a total of $25,000 in the budget year for expenses exceeding the provincial budget for the current year. If the sum exceeds $25,000, the consent of the Provincial Council must be obtained (LCO 590).

64.	We ORDAIN that the annual conventual budget approved by the House Council shall be the spending guide for the priors and other local superiors. Priors and local superiors may spend or grant permission to spend up to a total of $2,000 in the budget year for expenses exceeding the conventual budget. If the sum exceeds $2,000, the matter must be submitted to the House Council for approval. If the sum exceeds $25,000 in the budget year the matter must be submitted to the Prior Provincial (LCO 590).

65.	We COMMISSION the Provincial Syndic, with either the Economic Council of the Province or a subcommittee of the Provincial Council, to provide an accurate and concise accounting of the debt in order to determine the necessity of the 5% increase in Provincial tax ordained by the Provincial Chapter of 2011.

66.	We ORDAIN that the Prior Provincial with the support of 2/3 of his Council reduce the Provincial tax to 20% sooner than the next Provincial Chapter should it be determined that the reduction is fiscally feasible.

Intellectual Life

67. Aquinas Institute of Theology serves the Province as its center for institutional studies in the academic formation of our clerical and cooperator brothers. One of our provincial priorities, if not the first priority, it makes possible a future for the Province. The Province, in its ownership of Aquinas Institute, must clearly state the purpose and goals of Aquinas Institute, revise our constitutional and governmental structures in such a way that the Province may have a greater impact upon its future direction, and renew our support of it with personnel, with finances and with the self-sacrifice required to allow it to flourish.

Aquinas Institute of Theology

68. We DECLARE that, in response to Recommendation #2 in the Visitation Letter of the Master of the Order (December 1, 2014), the Nineteenth Provincial Chapter of the Province of St. Albert the Great, U.S.A., discussed the "purpose and goals of Aquinas Institute of Theology in its service to the Church"; thus, the primary purpose of Aquinas Institute is the academic formation of our clerical and cooperator brothers for the Provinces of St. Albert the Great and St. Martin de Porres. Aquinas Institute also educates for ministry other seminarians, religious and lay students, who qualify for admittance to the programs offered by Aquinas Institute.

69. We ORDAIN that, in response to Recommendation #2 in the Visitation Letter of the Master of the Order (Dec 1, 2014), within six months after the approval of the Acta, the Provincial with his Council appoint an appropriate brother to guide discussions regarding Aquinas Institute in each local

community or geographical area.

Constitutional and Provincial Structures Related to the Intellectual Life

70.   We ORDAIN that, in response to Recommendation #3 in the Visitation Letter of the Master of the Order (December 1, 2014), the Regent of Studies shall be appointed Modera-tor of the Center of Institutional Studies in accord with LCO 92-bis; and, in accord with LCO 93 § I.2, he shall be respon-sible for all academic advising of Dominican brothers at Aquinas Institute, thus assuming the former role of Aca-demic Advisor for Dominican brothers.

71.   We ORDAIN that the position of Academic Advisor for Dominican Students shall be abolished.

72.   We ORDAIN that in addition to the duties listed in LCO 93 §I [see also Statute 21], the Prior Provincial and his Council, as Members of the Corporation of Aquinas Insti-tute of Theology, seek ways, according to the governance and administrative structures of Aquinas Institute of Theology, to insure that the Regent of Studies shall, *ex officio*, be constituted as a member of the faculty of Aquinas Institute of Theology. He would only receive a salary if he is teaching at the Institute.

73.   We RECOMMEND that the Regent of Studies ordinarily live in a community of brothers in St. Louis.

74.   We RECALL to the attention to the Regent of Studies and the Intellectual Life Commission to act as advisors to the administration and faculty of Aquinas Institute of Theology, giving special attention to the implementation of the *Ratio Studiorum Generalis*, the *Ratio Studiorum Particularis*, and the *Program of Priestly Formation* of the United States Catholic Conference of Bishops [Cf. RSP 2004, n.99].

75. We RECALL to the attention of the Regent of Studies and the Intellectual Life Commission to utilize the procedures in the *Ratio Studiorum Particularis* (2004) and the *Faculty Handbook of Aquinas Institute of Theology [3.3.4]*.

76. We ORDAIN that, in addition to the duties listed in LCO 89 § III and 251-bis and 251-ter, the Promoter of Permanent Formation shall have special care and concern for all aspects of permanent formation after the years of initial formation are concluded, especially for:
    a. The organization and coordination of a yearly program of ongoing formation for priors/superiors and lectors;
    b. Assisting brothers who apply for programs of ongoing formation;
    c. Supervising and coordinating programs for those brothers who are transitioning into ministry for the first time or are transitioning from one ministry to another (e.g. Dominican Integrative Gathering [DIG]).

77. We ORDAIN that, for the sake of information and convenience, "job descriptions" of the Intellectual Life Commission, the Promoter of Permanent Formation, and the Regent of Studies, as provided in *The Book of Constitutions and Ordinations* and specified by Provincial Statute and the Acta of the Nineteenth Provincial Chapter, be appended to the Acta of the Chapter.

Initial Formation

78. We ORDAIN that upon the promulgation of the new *Ratio Studiorum Generalis* and the *Ratio Formationis Generalis* (both expected in 2016), the Prior Provincial and the Regent of Studies of the Province of Saint Albert the Great, in conjunction with the Prior Provincial and the Regent of Studies of the Province of Saint Martin de Porres, shall initiate a process to create a joint *Ratio Formationis Particularis* and a joint *Ratio Studiorum Particularis*

Novitiate

79.   We RECALL to the attention of the Regent of Studies [RSP 2004, n.13] to see to it that novices are instructed by the Master of Novices or by someone appointed by him in the following specific study components:

    a.   The theological foundations of the evangelical counsels;

    b.   An introduction to the theology of liturgy and spirituality as well as their histories; Dominican spirituality and the investigation of varied prayer forms;

    c.   An introduction to the study of the theology of ministry and, specifically, areas of particular import as delineated by the Province's statutes and stated priorities;

    d.   The study of the nature, theology, and history of religious life;

    e.   Studies in the history of Dominican thought and spirituality, in the life and thought of Dominicans outstanding in the Sacred Disciplines, most notably St. Thomas Aquinas and St. Catherine of Siena;

    f.   An investigation into the role of the intellectual life through the consideration of the Constitutions and Ordinations of the Order, the *Ratio Studiorum Generalis*, the *Ratio Studiorum Particularis* and supplemental readings in the life of study;

    g.   A general program of study of Catholic doctrine; and

    h.   Exercises fostering individual psychological development and communication. [Cf. LCO 187]

Studentate

80.   We COMMISSION the Regent of Studies and the Intellectual Life Commission to determine how the philosophy requirements of the *Ratio Studiorum Generalis* and the *Ratio Studiorum Particularis* of the Province might be fulfilled within the first two years of initial formation. The Regent and the Commission should take special note of the *Decree on the Reform of Ecclesiastical Studies of Philosophy* (28 January

2011) of the Congregation for Catholic Education.

81.	We ORDAIN that the Regent of Studies and the Intellectual Life Commission in consultation with the local formation council shall create a plan to identify brothers to pursue higher studies in order to provide the necessary professors and specialists for the Center of Institutional Studies for the Province and for the academic institutions under the immediate jurisdiction of the Master of the Order.

82.	We EXHORT the Regent to implement the Spanish language requirement of the *Ratio Studiorum Particularis* (#56.1; cf. Acts 2011, #42).

New Priory Press

83.	We ORDAIN that our Prior Provincial with his Council shall establish an editorial board to direct the future work of New Priory Press and shall delineate its responsibilities.

84.	We RECOMMEND that the Prior Provincial and his Council discuss hiring a full-time lay professional for New Priory Press should a friar not be available full-time.

LEADERSHIP

85.	Input from the January 2015 provincial assembly coupled with information from Dominic Perri of the Essential Conversations Group led to the dissemination of a provincial survey on Leadership Skills in preparation for the June 2015 Provincial Chapter. Analysis noted that brothers felt they had sufficient spiritual and theological training, but lacked some practical skills that were central to their ministries. There was also great concern for brothers transitioning from initial formation to full time ministry.

Leadership Formation

86. We COMMISSION the Prior Provincial with his Council to form an *ad hoc* committee to create a plan for leadership development. The plan shall incorporate the mission of the province and seek to provide every brother with an opportunity to grow in the following areas:
    a. To lead and collaborate with teams (either teams of Dominicans or lay people)
    b. To manage (i.e. human resources and office management)
    c. To elicit feedback on a brother's effectiveness in leadership and his areas for growth
    d. To resolve conflict in the ministry site or community
    e. To acquire a greater understanding and skills in budgeting and finance

87. We EXHORT the promoter of vocations to discern the leadership capacity of aspirants to the Order. Likewise, we urge formators to cultivate in the novices and students various qualities and virtues necessary for leadership.

88. We RECOMMEND that members in leadership positions in the province participate in The Pastor's Toolbox, Catholic Leadership 360, Amazing Parish, or similar programs within the first year of assignment.

Promoter of Permanent Formation

89. We ORDAIN that, in addition to the duties listed in LCO 89 § III and 251-bis and 251 -ter, the promoter of permanent formation shall foster leadership by:
    Creating a curriculum for the Dominican Integrative Gathering (DIG), or its equivalent, by July 1, 2016 to facilitate the transition to full time ministry and strengthen leadership skills.

90.   We COMMISSION the promoter of permanent formation, in addition to the duties listed in LCO 89 § III and 251-bis and 251-ter, to foster leadership by:
Generating a list of professional mentors, coaches, and programs that brothers can utilize when they are in need of support in ministry;
Working in conjunction with the Prior Provincial to connect a brother with a friar mentor in his first assignment after initial formation;
Creating a curriculum developing necessary skills to be a friar mentor.

Leadership Transitions

91.   We RECOMMEND that the Prior Provincial, when assigning a brother to a new ministry, make available the appro-priate resources, support, and mentoring to help in the transition.

92.   We RECOMMEND that the Prior Provincial consider equally the community and ministry when assigning a brother to a new assignment, especially at the beginning of a brother's first years of ministry after initial formation.

93.   We RECOMMEND that the Prior Provincial ordinarily assign brothers to new communities when their terms as pastors or provincial leaders are completed.

Leadership in Common Life

94.   We RECOMMEND that the Prior Provincial meet quarterly with priors and superiors via telecommunications or other forms of social media with a goal to strengthen our communities.

95.   We RECOMMEND that priors and superiors help lead the spiritual renewal of our Dominican life by:
a.   Encouraging brothers to not easily dispense themselves

from prayer in common and other spiritual practices (ACG Trogir #65);

b. Incorporating into community meetings spiritual reflections on the scripture;

c. Providing for the celebration of a conventual Mass at least once a week (LCO 59 §1);

d. Encouraging brothers to take the initiative in strengthening practices of regular observance (LCO 39, 40).

Petition

96. We PETITION the Master of the Order to consider including discussions on leadership development and transition in ministry at the next General Chapter.

GOVERNMENT

Holy Rosary-Santo Rosario Parish

97. We RECOMMEND that the Province continue to commit to Minneapolis as a center for ministry into the future.

98. We RECOMMEND that the Province commit to continue providing Holy Rosary-Santo Rosario Church with a full-time dedicated Spanish-speaking priest.

We COMMISSION the Provincial Syndic to enter into conversation with Holy Rosary-Santo Rosario Parish regarding the repair of the roof of the church with a view toward investigating all possible alternatives, with a decision to be made by 1 September 2015 so work can begin before the winter.

Denver Priory Project

99. We COMMISSION the Prior Provincial with his Council to authorize the payment of the necessary funds (already allocated) for the completion of Phase I of the Denver Priory Project.

100. We COMMISSION the Prior Provincial with his Council, after receiving all the reports from Phase I of the Denver Priory Project:
    a. To determine the advisability of authorizing Phase II of the Project;
    b. To make any necessary revisions of the scope of the project; and
    c. To set the financial parameters of the project no later than 30 October 2015.

Revised Statutes

101. We ORDAIN that, in response to Recommendation #9 in the Visitation Letter of the Master of the Order (Dec 1, 2014), Statute 53, 2 shall be replaced with the following text:

    The Provincial Economic Council shall consist of the following persons: the Syndic of the Province, *ex officio*, who serves as Chair, the Vicar for Mission Advancement, *ex officio*, at least one other brother, and at least two lay persons with expertise in finances. Members are appointed by the Prior Provincial with his Council. The Council shall meet at least twice a year. Terms shall be four years [LCO 581. 1]

102. We ORDAIN that Statute 21, paragraph 2, of the Province shall be amended to read:

    21. The Regent has the duties listed in LCO 93, I (Avila, n.99, I), must have the qualifications listed in LCO 93, II (Avila, n.99, II), and is appointed as

specified in LCO 93, III (Oakland, n.214). In addition he is, ex officio, a member of the Board of Trustees of Aquinas Institute, a member of the faculty of Aquinas Institute (without salary unless he is actually engaged in teaching at Aquinas Institute), and a member of the Academic Council of Aquinas Institute. He may be reappointed once. It is desirable that the term of the Regent of Studies begin with the term of the newly-elected Provincial. [81/18; 85/87; 90/39; 15/ 98]

103.　　We ORDAIN that Statute 22 of the Province shall be amended to read:

> 22. The Regent of Studies shall be assisted by the Intellectual Life Commission of which he is chairman, *ex officio*. It shall include the Promoter of Permanent Formation, *ex officio*, and at least four other brothers appointed by the Provincial Chapter or the Prior Provincial with his Council, according to the norms of LCO 89 (Rome, n.313). Appointed members of the Commission shall serve a four-year term on a rotating basis. [81/82; 85/88; 15/ 99].

104.　　We ORDAIN that Statute 23, II, of the Province shall be amended to read:

> II. The Regent of Studies in consultation with the Dominican brothers on the faculty of the Center of Institutional Studies of the Province shall guide and encourage student and cooperator brothers who wish to pursue doctoral studies. The names of those with promise and interest shall be sent to the Intellectual Life Commission.

105.　　We ORDAIN that Statute 24 of the Province shall be amended to read:

COMMENDATIONS

106. We COMMEND both *our* former Bolivian Vicariate and the Bolivian Vicariate of Teutonia for successfully unifying and achieving the status of Vice Province. We CONGRAT-ULATE our brother, Jorge Saldias Pedraza, O.P., on his appointment as Auxiliary Bishop of La Paz, Bolivia.

107. We COMMEND our brother, Nicholas Monco, O.P., for his work with social media in evangelization with his *Harry Potter* series.

108. We COMMEND our brother, Albert Judy, O.P., for his work in translating the sermons of St. Vincent Ferrer into English.

109. We COMMEND our past Prior Provincial, Charles Bouchard, O.P., and his Council, for establishing New Priory Press.

110. We COMMEND our brothers, Albert Judy, O.P. and Andrew McAlpin, O.P., for their work in editing and preparing texts for publication for New Priory Press.

111. We COMMEND our brother, Donald Goergen, O.P., for his service as Academic Advisor for Dominican Students and especially for his efforts to collaborate with the Philosophy Department of Saint Louis University toward establishing a sound philosophy program for our students.

112. We COMMEND our brothers, Michael Mascari, O.P., Albert Glade, O.P., Dominic Holtz, O.P., and Michael Monshau, O.P., for their service to the Order both in the General Curia and at the Pontifical University of St. Thomas Aquinas (Angelicum) in Rome.

113. We COMMEND our brother, David Wright, O.P., for his work in preparing the annual Liturgical Calendar.

114. We COMMEND Aquinas Institute of Theology for identifying and incorporating a strong leadership component into the M.Div. program.

115. We COMMEND our past Prior Provincial, Charles Bouchard, O.P., and the *ad hoc* Liturgical Commission for their on-going work in revising and publishing the Grail version of the Liturgy of the Hours.

116. We COMMEND our past Prior Provincial, Charles Bouchard, O.P., for his leadership with the Fenwick High School Board of Directors by updating the bylaws, creating a new board structure, and forming a new administrative leadership team.

117. We COMMEND our past Prior Provincial, Charles Bouchard, O.P., Andrew Carl Wisdom, O.P., and Mr. Bob Dixon, Director of the Office for Mission Advancement, for their work in advancing and improving our development efforts.

CONCLUSION

Suffrages for the Living

118. For Pope Francis, for Pope Emeritus Benedict XVI, for the College of Cardinals, for the Synod of Bishops, and for the National Conference of Bishops, each of community shall celebrate one Mass.

For the Master of the Order, for the General Council of the Order, and for the welfare of the Order throughout the world, each community shall celebrate one Mass.

For the Prior Provincial, for the provincial administration, and for the welfare of the entire Province, each community shall celebrate one Mass.

For an increase in vocations, for those who are experiencing difficulty in their vocation, for those who have departed from our brotherhood, each community shall celebrate one Mass.

For all our friends, relatives, and benefactors, and for the intentions of all those whom we serve, each community shall celebrate one Mass.

Suffrages for the Dead

119. For all the deceased members of our Province and the Order, for all our deceased friends, relatives, and benefactors, and for all the faithful departed, each priest shall celebrate one Mass and each clerical and cooperator brother shall participate in one Mass for the same intention.

Assignment of the next Provincial Chapter

120. The next ordinary Provincial Chapter (twentieth) shall be held at St. Pius V Priory, Chicago, Illinois, beginning in June, 2019, on a day to be determined by the Prior Provincial with his Council.

121. These are the Acts of the Nineteenth Provincial Chapter of the Province of Saint Albert the Great, in the United States of America, celebrated in the Convent of Saint Dominic, St. Louis, Missouri, from June 11 until June 24, 2015. Once approved and published, these Acts along with the legislation approved by the Eighteenth Provincial Chapter, are to be read and studied by each brother and then discussed in every community of the Province in community meetings convened by the prior or superior for this purpose. This shall be done as soon as possible after the reception of these Acts.

Given at the Convent of Saint Dominic in St. Louis, Missouri, under the seal of the Province, on this 24th day of the month of June in the year of our Lord 2015.

James V. Marchionda, O.P.
Prior Provincial

David Wright, O.P.
1st Diffinitor

Kevin Nichols, O.P.
2nd Diffinitor

Leonardo Altuzan, O.P.
3rd Diffinitor

Paul Byrd, O.P.
4th Diffinitor

SEAL

Raymond Bryce, O.P.
Secretary

APPENDIX A

Dominican City Centers

In looking at the signs of the times, it appears the greatest need in the Church today is for evangelization and the creation of disciples, especially among the young. As Dominicans, we are uniquely gifted to respond to this call. In doing so, we must be mindful of the primary importance of witness in evangelization. The way we live our lives is our primary preaching. Therefore, we must balance our emphasis on ministry with a robust living of the regular life, especially our communal life (praying and simply living together as brothers, as family). Further, as an Order based on study, we have a responsibility to act as the brain cells in the body of Christ and reach out in dialogue with the world today. In addition, we need to go to where people are rather than waiting for them to come to us, itinerantly seeking out the margins.

However, if we are to respond effectively, we need to focus: we cannot do everything. We are going to have to make sacrifices and get smaller before we get bigger: better to do a few things well than many so-so (or even poorly). Specifically, we need to focus on creating Dominican City Centers. Rather than seeing our Province as a series of ministries, we should think of our presence in cities and dioceses, and ask ourselves the question: "What are we as Dominicans called to do in this city?" We must see ourselves at the service of the broader Church, and not be overly focused on individual ministries. These City Centers would be larger communities (eight to twelve friars) so as to enable the common life. Following the principle of subsidiarity, this effort would require a dialogue between the local ordinary, the Province, and the local community. Ultimately, these Dominican City Centers would focus on evangelizing and providing faith formation, since a large part of our work will be forming the lay evangelizers on the front lines.

More concretely, here is a description of a sample Dominican City Center, including examples of the types of ministries the friars could take on:

- Centered around a university
- Priory would be near the university
- Prayer life of the community would take place at the university, offered as a form of prayer for students and also for the whole city
- 2-3 friars working for campus ministry
- 2-3 friars working as professors at university (perhaps overlap with previous)
- Take on an urban parish
- Minimum of 3 friars assigned
- Especially, but not exclusively, geared towards young adults who are repopulating cities across the country
- Opportunity for outreach to the poor and marginalized
- Center for confessions for the city (all priests in community can help)
- Offer instruction in preaching to priests of the diocese
- Itinerant preaching team resides here
- Itinerant teachers: teach theology courses for credit at secular universities in/near the city through religious studies programs, open to anybody in the area; perhaps teaching through "satellite programs" would be easier to manage
- Summer retreat program: for people looking for something more substantial than entry-level retreats, which is usually all lay people are given
- This would be open to people in the whole city or region, not just our parishes
- Set up a center for Lay Faith Formation in which all friars teach actual theology courses
- A service to the whole diocese: people need not be our parishioners, but can come here for more substantial faith formation
- Not a certificate or degree-seeking program; free, but donation encouraged

- Additional brothers can work at chancery (e.g., canon lawyers, Evangelization Office, Diaconate Formation program, etc.), serve as hospital chaplains, high school chaplains or teachers, etc.
- Parish supply
- Older brothers can serve as wisdom figures and anchors for the community

STATUTES OF THE
PROVINCE OF ST. ALBERT THE GREAT, U.S.A.

This section contains all of the Statutes of the Province of St. Albert the Great, U.S.A., listed in the approved Acts of previous Provincial Chapters with all amendments, deletions, and additions enacted by the Nineteenth Provincial Chapter (2015) of the Province.

I. RELIGIOUS CONSECRATION

1.   The Prior Provincial shall provide for a daily Eucharist to be celebrated for the welfare of our Province. The Eucharist is to be celebrated frequently in all our houses for our benefactors, both living and deceased. [69/37; 73/2; 90/45]

2.   Each assignment is to be of sufficient duration to promote the work of the brethren effectively, and to provide for the formation of a true community. However, the assignment should not ordinarily exceed twelve years in a single geographic location (cf. Oakland, n. 39). [69/39; 90/46]

3.   With the approval of the Prior Provincial, as an exceptional situation and with an annual review by the Prior Provincial or his delegate, a brother may be permitted to live alone. He should be assigned, however, to a particular and proximate community within the Province and should be mindful of his share in community obligations.

       Both he and his community shall faithfully fulfill their mutual responsibilities toward their respective spiritual, psychological, social, and material needs. [73/3; 77/23]

4.   All professed members in a local community shall be convened at least once a month on a given regular date, with priority over all other meetings. The community meeting is to have a planned agenda, with the superior or an appointed

facilitator presiding. Prayer should be part of every meeting (see LCO 7, I). [73/10; 85/54; 90/48]

5. Local communities under the leadership of the prior or local superior shall formulate their own norms to provide the witness of religious poverty to their surroundings, to maintain firmly the principle of common possessions and financial accountability and to avoid private life among the brethren. [69/43; 90/49; 94/49]

6. The limits of the enclosure shall be determined by the needs of the local community (LCO 41). [69/44; 73/6; 85/55]

7. If we are to become effective preachers of the Word, silence is absolutely necessary (LCO 46). The determining factor for specific times and places for the observance of silence ought to be the activities of the brethren. External silence shall be observed diligently in our communities, especially in times and places destined for prayer, study, and rest. Other determinations regarding silence as to time and place shall be made by the community chapter according to the traditions of the Order. [73/6.01]

8. In addition to provisions of ecclesiastical law, each member and each community of the Province shall observe a special day of prayer, almsgiving, fast and abstinence for peace and social justice during the seasons of Advent and Lent. Other penitential practices, especially during the time of Lent, shall be left to the discretion of the local community.

Also, frequently during the year and especially at the beginning of Lent, each brother and each community shall examine the simplicity of their individual and communal styles of life. At these times, each community shall determine a sum of money to be given to the poor.

When performed in a spirit of fraternal service, the sharing of domestic tasks, regular attendance at community meetings, and ready availability to others in the ministry are effective contemporary forms of penance. [73/6.02; 85/56]

9.   The brethren are to dress at all times in conformity with their religious calling, professional status, and ordinary good manners. The Dominican habit shall be worn as prudence dictates according to local circumstances (LCO 51). [69/47]

10. Upon the death of a member of the immediate family of one of our brothers, the house to which he is assigned is to communicate information about funeral arrangements to the Provincial Office which will then notify the rest of the Province. [73/11]

11. Individuals and communities shall deal directly with the problems of our brothers who become alcoholic or chemically dependent according to the accepted norm of the Policy on Chemical Dependency and Alcoholism. [77/24]

12. The Policy on Aging and Limited Service shall stand as the accepted norm of the Province, subject to review and revision by a Provincial Chapter. [77/25; 81/63]

13. All affiliated members of St. Albert's Province shall be eligible for participation in the Province's programs of continuing education, major medical insurance, and aging and limited service, and they shall observe the taxation policies established for the brothers of the Province. [77/26; 81/116]

14. The house chapter and local superior shall bear primary responsibility for promoting and encouraging the common life and, when necessary, shall confront charitably those members of the community who exempt themselves from this obligation. Only when the community's efforts have failed, should the matter be referred to the Prior Provincial. The Prior Provincial, with or without members of the Council,

shall confront charitably the local community when it fails to fulfill this duty. (See "Dominican Community," Appendix II, 1977 ACTS.) [85/66]

II. LITURGY AND PRAYER

15. Because of the importance of the community Eucharist in our lives, it should be celebrated regularly and at a time when the greater number of the brethren can be present. At these celebrations a homily is to be preached based on the text of Sacred Scripture. [69/56; 73/19; 85/57]

16. The Sacrament of Penance must be recognized as a valuable means of continuing Christian conversion. Forms of communal penance are encouraged. We strongly encourage penance services in our communities, particularly during the seasons of Advent and Lent. [69/63; 73/23; 90/50]

17. Because the Eucharist is mirrored in the ordinary meals of Christians, the main meal of the day in our communities should be appropriately blessed by prayer. This should not be a perfunctory formula, but a prayer reflecting the liturgical character of the day and recalling the community to a sense of their meal's meaning and importance. [69/61; 85/59]

18. Recitation of the rosary in common is not required. However, communities are encouraged to use not only the traditional form of the rosary but also new approved forms (LCO 67, II). [73/23.01; 85/60]

19. The individual's responsibility to make a retreat each year is reaffirmed (LCO 68). It is the community's responsibility to provide financial resources for retreats. Local communities should encourage spiritual enrichment through days of recollection. [77/41; 90/51]

III. INTELLECTUAL LIFE

20. All ministries of the Church which accord with the fundamental goals of our Order are open to any of our brethren, clerical or cooperator, in ways consistent with their state, when they are properly prepared. Every brother shall be provided, to the limit set by Provincial resources, with all educational opportunities fitted to his talents, gifts, and ministry. These opportunities are to include:
    1. the basic philosophical and theological education he needs to participate fully in the life and ministry of our communities;
    2. the special education he needs to perform his ministry;
    3. continuing education by which he can achieve life-long personal and professional growth. [73/41; 85/86]

21. The Regent of Studies, under the authority of the Prior Provincial and with the counsel of the Intellectual Life Commission, is responsible for the promotion and coordination of the entire intellectual life of the Province (see Rome, n.317, and LCO 93, I).

    The Regent has the duties listed in LCO 93, I (Avila, n. 99, I), must have the qualifications listed in LCO 93, II (Avila, n. 99, II), and is appointed as specified in LCO 93, III (Oakland, n. 214). He may be reappointed once. It is desirable that the term of the Regent of Studies begin with the term of the newly-elected Provincial. [81/18; 85/87; 90/39]

    Statute 21, paragraph 2, of the Province shall be amended to read:

    > The Regent has the duties listed in LCO 93, I (Avila, n.99, I), must have the qualifications listed in LCO 93, II (Avila, n.99, II), and is appointed as specified in LCO 93, III (Oakland, n.214). In addition he is, *ex officio,* a member of the Board of Trustees of Aquinas Institute,

a member of the faculty of Aquinas Institute (without salary unless he is actually engaged in teaching at Aquinas Institute), and a member of the Academic Council of Aquinas Institute. He may be reappointed once. It is desirable that the term of the Regent of Studies begin with the term of the newly-elected Provincial. [81/18; 85/87; 90/39; 15/ 98]

22. The Regent of Studies shall be assisted by the Intellectual Life Commission of which he is chairman. It shall include the Promoter of Permanent Formation, the President of Aquinas Institute of Theology, the Academic Adviser for Dominican Students, and at least four other brothers appointed by the Provincial Chapter or the Prior Provincial and the Council, according to the norms of LCO 89 (Rome, n. 313). Appointed members of the Commission shall serve a four-year term on a rotating basis. [81/82; 85/88]

Statute 22 of the Province shall be amended to read:

The Regent of Studies shall be assisted by the Intellectual Life Commission of which he is chairman, *ex officio*. It shall include the Promoter of Permanent Formation, *ex officio*, and at least four other brothers appointed by the Provincial Chapter or the Prior Provincial with his Council, according to the norms of LCO 89 (Rome, n.313). Appointed members of the Commission shall serve a four-year term on a rotating basis. [81/82; 85/88; 15/ 99].

23. Because of the importance to all the apostolates of the Province and to the Church that there be experts in the areas of theology and the allied disciplines, it is necessary that there should be a process of discernment of the intellectual needs of the Province and the gifts and abilities of the brothers. Therefore:

I. The Regent and the Intellectual Life Commission, considering the intellectual needs of the Province and of the Church, shall initiate a process through which the names of brothers who might be suited and inclined to doctoral studies can be identified, that is, they shall take the initiative in the recruitment of men to pursue advanced studies.

II. The Academic Adviser for Dominican Students at the Center of Basic Studies of the Province and the Dominicans on the faculty shall guide and encourage student brothers who wish to pursue doctoral studies. The names of those with promise and interest shall be sent to the Intellectual Life Commission.

Statute 23, II, of the Province shall be amended to read:

II. The Regent of Studies in consultation with the Dominican brothers on the faculty of the Center of Institutional Studies of the Province shall guide and encourage student and cooperator brothers who wish to pursue doctoral studies. The names of those with promise and interest shall be sent to the Intellectual Life Commission.

III. The Intellectual Life Commission shall investigate sources of institutional funding for members of the Province, making this information available to those seriously planning doctoral, post-doctoral, or research projects. [85/89]

24.   The Center of Basic Studies for the Province of St. Albert the Great shall be Aquinas Institute of Theology (St. Louis, Missouri), which is also a center of higher studies and pastoral disciplines. [85/90]

Statute 24 of the Province shall be amended to read:

The Center of Institutional Studies for the Province...

25. The offices of Regent of Studies and President of Aquinas Institute of Theology shall be incompatible. [85/91]

26. Aquinas Institute of Theology shall be governed by its own bylaws, which specify that the Prior Provincial and the Council constitute the Members of the Aquinas Institute Corporation with ultimate authority over the Institute. The Prior Provincial and the Council shall have power to elect an operating Board of Directors other than themselves should they so decide. The President of Aquinas Institute of Theology shall be appointed by the Members and shall be responsible to them. [85/92]

27. Priors and superiors shall assure that the function of the conventual lector is fulfilled in their communities. The conventual lector is elected by the conventual chapter for a three-year term and is confirmed by the Prior Provincial. The offices of prior or superior and conventual lector are not incompatible. The Prior Provincial and the Council may assign further duties other than those contained in LCO 326 bis, II. [85/93]

IV. MINISTRY OF THE WORD

28. Our ministries often require resources beyond those available to the individual or the local community. We are to be willing give support and approval to each other in our various ministries, provided that continuing evaluation gives evidence that they are meeting real pastoral needs. Local communities, as well as the Province, can support the ministries of individuals or of other communities by offering financial aid or housing facilities, and by encouraging brethren to join in these ministries. [73/58]

29.	The Province itself, and individual brothers when possible, are to have a written agreement relative to their ministerial commitments with the diocese or institution involved. This written agreement shall include a statement of mutual obligations, a renewal date, and a provision for re-evaluation and re-negotiation at a specified time. [73/60]

30.	I. Within the Province there shall be the following:
	A.	a Promoter of Preaching;
	B.	a Promoter of Social Justice and a Commission on Social Justice;
	C.	a Director of the Shrine of St. Jude Thaddeus [90/1; 94/108; 03/116]

	II. The promoters or directors and the commissions or committees are appointed for their various terms by the Provincial Chapter or the Prior Provincial and the Council.

V. BASIC FORMATION

31.	First profession is ordinarily made for two years. It must then be renewed either for one year, to complete three years (LCO 195, II; Canon 655) or, if the brother's initial formation program includes a pastoral year, for two years to complete a total of four years. [85/65; 90/69; 94/58]

VI. GOVERNMENT

A. General Statutes

32.	In addition to the provincial officials required by the Constitutions, the Provincial Chapter or the Prior Provincial and the Council may institute such officials as are necessary to strive for the goals of the Province. The work of these officials shall be explained to the Province (LCO 380). [81/122]

33. Preserving the liberty of the Prior Provincial and the Council, all Provincial Council meetings shall be open to all the brothers. A call for executive session insures the privacy and liberty of Council members. Further, a summary of the minutes of Council meetings, together with a record of how each member votes on each issue – minutes and votes of executive sessions being excepted – is to be publicized to members of the Province. [81/120]

34. The competent superior for accepting a parish is the Prior Provincial with the consent of the Provincial Council; the Provincial Chapter has not reserved this right to itself (LCO 128, III). [73/94; 90/96]

35. Saving the rights of the local ordinary and the Provincial, the "Guidelines on Parish and Campus Ministries" shall stand as accepted norms of the Province, subject to review by a Provincial Chapter. [99/133]

36. More serious decisions concerning community life, apostolic work, and economic administration, shall require a decisive vote of the community chapter. [69/128]

37. The rights and duties of brethren living outside of a priory or non-prioral community shall be the same as those residing in the community, saving the provision of Statute 39. [73/90.02]

38. The brethren mentioned in LCO 458, II, shall retain active voice in the election of a prior unless they be absent from the priory for more than a total of six months during the twelve months preceding the election. The time shall be determined by the president of the election. [73/91.01; 99/128]

39. A month before leaving office, each prior or house superior shall render an account of his administration to the conventual chapter or house chapter and to the Prior

Provincial according to the standard form furnished by the Prior Provincial (LCO 306). [73/95.01; 90/96; 03/95]

40. Ordinarily, the positions of pastor and house superior shall be held by different brothers due to the distinct qualifications for and responsibilities of each office. [03/96; 07/110]

41. When the Prior Provincial ceases to hold office in accord with LCO 344, I, the Vicar of the Province will be the prior of the convent where the Provincial Chapter will be held, and if this convent lacks a prior, the prior of the house where the last Chapter was celebrated (LCO 348, I). [69/133]

42. At least a three-year period of assignment to our Province shall be required before the Prior Provincial and the Council consider the request of a brother for transfiliation from another province of the Order. [77/110]

43. To insure the continuity of the work of permanent boards, committees, councils, and commissions, the appointed members shall serve on a rotating basis. Unless otherwise provided, the chairman shall be elected by the membership. [81/118; 85/116]

B. Statutes for Provincial Chapters

44. The Provincial Chapter shall be conducted according to the Constitutions of the Order with the following particular prescriptions (LCO 357):

   I. Pre-Chapter Commissions, consisting of delegates and other members of the Province chosen through nomination by members of the Province, shall be formed by the Prior Provincial and the Council at least three months before the beginning of the Chapter. Members of the Pre-Chapter Commissions who are not Chapter delegates cannot serve as chairmen of

Pre-Chapter Commissions, but can vote in all Commission deliberations. The final meetings of the Pre-Chapter Commissions shall be held on the eve of the Chapter in the convent where the Chapter will be celebrated. These Commissions may form subcommittees, if necessary (LCO 357.1). [77/96; 81/110; 07/110]

II. The election of the Prior Provincial shall take place no sooner than the fourth working day and no later than the eighth working day, the exact day to be determined by the vocals within the first two days (LCO 357.2). [77/100; 99/129; 07/110]

III. Four diffinitors shall be elected on the day after the election of the Prior Provincial (LCO 357.3). [69/140; 73/100; 77/101; 07/110]

IV. The election of three councilors and two alternate councilors and the election of the diffinitors and socii for the General Chapters shall be held at the time determined by the Chapter Committee (LCO 357.4 & 5). [77/102; 81/114; 85/115; 99/129; 07/110]

45.   Without prejudice to LCO 356.2, and 358, III, 1, the outgoing Prior Provincial and Provincial Council shall determine the officials who will report to the Provincial Chapter and the report format. [73/90; 77/103; 81/132; 90/97; 94/89; 99/130; 07/110]

46.   Upon the publication of the ACTS of a Provincial Chapter, a copy shall be sent to each member of the Province. Communities shall then hold meetings to review the ACTS and the Provincial Statutes and to discuss ways in which these ACTS can be implemented in each of our houses. [94/50]

VII. ECONOMIC ADMINISTRATION

47.   I. The Prior Provincial and his Council shall determine and establish the rights of apostolates and our provincial institutions, projects, and commissions by making them subject to the Prior Provincial and independent of any community or local superior and by appointing qualified administrators who report to the provincial administration. The personnel of such apostolates and our provincial institutions, projects, and commissions shall make arrangements with the Prior Provincial and his Council, after consultation with their respective communities, to contribute to the financial help of their houses of assignment. [03/97]

II. The finances of our apostolates and our provincial institutions, projects, and commissions shall be separated from those of our communities and individuals. Both the Province and the community in which an independent apostolate, project, or institute is located shall receive its financial report and be informed of its activities. [69/177; 81/134; 85/125]

48.   Every priory and formal house shall be incorporated according to the laws of the state wherein possible (LCO 554). When it is advantageous, other apostolates and our provincial institutions, projects, and commissions should also be incorporated. The Syndic of the Province shall inspect the corporate records annually. A copy of the Articles of Incorporation and a copy of the annual report sent to the local state office are to be forwarded to the Syndic of the Province. [69/178; 73/137; 03/99]

49.   For the benefit of our common life and for reasons of civil law, all bank accounts used by and for members of the Province for community use, or by individuals living alone or having special ministries shall be corporate accounts. These accounts shall be in the name of the Province corporation or

of the local community corporation. In addition to the individual who normally administers the account, officers of the corporation which authorizes the account shall have signatory power. [85/128]

50. At least once a year a community chapter shall discuss the finances of the community, examine the most recent financial statement submitted to the Prior Provincial, and examine the budget for the following year. The budget and financial statement shall be submitted to the Prior Provincial within the first month of the fiscal year. (LCO 563, II). [69/178; 73/138; 77/129; 07/110]

51. When the Prior Provincial or his delegate conducts a canonical visitation of a community or individual, he consults with the Syndic of the Province beforehand in order to ascertain the extent to which the community or individual is acting in accord with the economic legislation and policies of the Order and the Province. If there are areas of noncompliance, the visitator shall address these at the visitation, if necessary with the assistance of the Syndic of the Province. [94/114]

52. The Prior Provincial and the Syndic of the Province shall be consulted concerning the administration of the goods of others. Permission for such administration shall be given in writing and only for a specified period of time. An annual report of such administration shall be made to the Prior Provincial and Syndic of the Province. If benefits are derived, they shall accrue to the Province. [73/144; 81/135]

53. I. Outside the time of the Provincial Chapter, it belongs to the Prior Provincial and the Council to appoint and remove the Syndic of the Province. His term ordinarily shall be four years, i.e., until appointment by the next Chapter. The Syndic of the Province shall be limited to two terms.

II. The Province Economic Council shall consist of seven

persons: the Syndic of the Province, as Chair, the Prior Provincial, at least three lay men or women with expertise in finances, and two other members from among the brethren. The Syndic and Prior Provincial serve *ex officio* and the other five members are appointed by the Prior Provincial with the consent of the Provincial Council. The Council shall meet at least twice a year. Terms shall be four years [LCO 581. I]

Statute 53, II shall be replaced with the following text:

> II. The Provincial Economic Council shall consist of the following persons: the Syndic of the Province, *ex officio*, who serves as Chair, the Vicar for Mission Advancement, *ex officio*, at least one other brother, and at least two lay persons with expertise in finances. Members are appointed by the Prior Provincial with his Council. The Council shall meet at least twice a year. Terms shall be four years [LCO 581. 1]

54. In accord with LCO 586, I, after consulting with the Provincial Economic Council, the Provincial Chapter shall provide the long-range economic plan of the Province regarding the expenditures for major projects. The total yearly budget for the Province shall be prepared by the Provincial Staff, reviewed by the Provincial Economic Council, and approved by the Prior Provincial and the Council. [73/145; 77/132]

55. Each year the Syndic of the Province shall send a clear and simple end-of-the-year financial report of the Province to every house and to every member living alone or living in Dominican Communities of other Provinces. This statement shall include a balance sheet, as well as a profit and loss statement for the fiscal year (LCO 577). [69/184; 77/133; 99/112; 03/101]

56. The standard forms regularly furnished by the Syndic of the

Province for reporting and recording financial information shall be used by each community, individual, institute, and project according to its own applicable circumstances and completed insofar as possible. [69/188; 73/147; 77/134]

57. With the aid of experts in the field, the Provincial Economic Council shall review periodically all insurance policies and shall direct changes in coverage as deemed necessary. [69/189; 73/148]

58. For insurance and tax reasons, all motor vehicles shall be titled to Dominicans, Province of St. Albert the Great, U.S.A., or to a legally incorporated local community, and not in the name of individual brothers. The insurance policy for all vehicles, whether owned or leased, must list the Province Corporation as an additionally named insured. [77/135]

59. Norms for Contracts:

I. A major business contract shall be considered any contract which exceeds the limitations as expressed in LCO 590.
   a. All major contracts shall be submitted for consultation to the Syndic of the Province and the Prior Provincial and the Council for approval.
   b. Once major contracts are made by the proper authorities no one has the right to make changes in this contract on his own authority (LCO 606). [69/187; 99/113]

II. Unless it is advantageous for a brother to enter directly into a contract with his employer for Social Security benefits, pension programs, etc., employment contracts and/or agreements with Catholic institutions shall be drawn up between the employer and the Province for the services of a particular brother. These contracts would necessarily be reviewed by the brother and signed by the Prior Provincial or his delegate on behalf of the Province. [07/110]

60. A qualified brother, designated by the Prior Provincial and his Council, shall assist our authors in negotiating contracts including a testamentary clause and promoting the sale of books or other electronic forms should be borne by the local community to which the author belongs. If the author is transferred to another community, the community which incurred the expenses should be reimbursed to the full extent out of royalties and thereafter the royalties accrue to his new house of assignment. On the death of the author, all royalties go to the Province. Exceptions should be negotiated through the Prior Provincial and his Council [LCO 546]. A copy of copyrights of books, electronic forms, and contracts with publishers is to be given to the Syndic of the Province to be kept in his file.

61. A Limited Service Fund is to be maintained in addition to the Qualified Church Pension Plan as a Quasi-endowment Fund to support those members of the Province who do not qualify for eligibility in the Church Pension Plan or who are in need of assistance beyond the benefit received from the Qualified Church Pension Plan. [99/114]

62. Provincial funds shall be invested according to the "Investment Policy Statement" and "Socially Responsible Guidelines for Investments" for each investment portfolio. These policies and guidelines shall be reviewed and revised by the Prior Provincial and the Council when deemed necessary. [81/137; 07/110]

63. All provincial fund-raising shall abide by the current norms established by the National Conference of Catholic Bishops (NCCB) and the National Catholic Development Conference (NCDC). [99/115]

Statute 63 shall be amended as follows:

All provincial fund-raising shall abide by the current norms established by the United States Conference of Catholic Bishops (USCCB) and the National Catholic Development Conference (NCDC). [99/115]

This Appendix contains brief biographies of all the members of the Province who have died since the Eighteenth Provincial Chapter in 2011. The following list is in alphabetical order. Biographies are given in chronological order according to dates of death.

Ashley, Benedict Winston	February 23, 2013
Baer, Benedict Gary	August 26, 2012
Botthof, Robert Jerome	October 15, 2014
Brown, Roderick Marvin	October 16, 2013
Cleary, Edward Louis	November 11, 2011
Dolehide, John Robert	July 26, 2012
Fabian, John Charles	October 29, 2014
Gerlach, John Harold	November 21, 2013
Hensley, Gilbert Leroy	May 31, 2014
Hoff, Wilfred Gabriel	July 18, 2014
Jagoe, Bede Robert	August 5, 2014
Kenny, Joseph Peter	January 28, 2011
Kyte, Michael Gerard	March 27, 2014
Morrison, Thomas Aquinas	April 1, 2014
Nouza, Francis Marcolinus	February 19, 2015
O'Rourke, Kevin David	March 28, 2012
Russell, Benjamin Joseph	August 11, 2014
Walsh, Matthias Jerome	November 3, 2013

EDWARD LOUIS CLEARY, O.P.

Edward Louis Cleary was born in Chicago, Illinois on August 4, 1929 to Emmet Vincent and Mary Veronica (Novotny) Cleary. He attended Marquette University, College of Journalism, in Milwaukee, Wisconsin. He entered the Novitiate August 30, 1950 at St. Peter Martyr Priory in Winona, Minnesota and was given the religious name of James. On August 31, 1951 he made first profession of vows. He attended the Dominican Houses of Studies in River Forest, Illinois, and Dubuque, Iowa, where he earned his bachelor's, licentiate and master's degrees in theology from the Aquinas Institute of Theology and was ordained a priest on May 25, 1957 at St. Rose Priory in Dubuque, Iowa. In 1975, he earned a Ph.D. in sociology from the University of Chicago.

Edward's first assignment was at San Geronimo Major Seminary in La Paz, Bolivia from 1958 to 1962 where he served as Professor of Philosophy and Theology, and as Director of Students. He also served at the Bolivian Institute for the Study of Social Action (IBEAS). In 1963, he returned to the United States to do campus ministry and to teach theology at St. Xavier's College in Chicago. In 1966, he was back in Bolivia to serve as Vicar Provincial of the Dominican Mission Vicariate in La Paz. From 1973 to 1976, he served at the University of Pittsburgh in Pennsylvania as Assistant Director of the Center for Latin American Studies. In 1976, he moved to St. Louis, Missouri to teach and to serve as Vice President/Academic Dean at the Aquinas Institute of Theology. In 1980, he became a research associate at the Institute of Latin American and Iberian Studies at Columbia University in New York, New York, and was a fellow at the Research Institute for the Study of Man, also in New York. From 1985 to 1993, he was director of the School of Theology Hispanic Ministries Program at the Pontifical College Josephinum in Columbus, Ohio.

In 1993, he began his career at Providence College in Providence, Rhode Island as a faculty member of the Latin

American Studies Program in the Department of Political Science, also serving as program director beginning in 1995. From the mid-1990s on, he organized and participated in many joint Providence College-US Naval War College student and faculty forums. He was a faculty affiliate of the Harvard University David Rockefeller Center for Latin American Studies in 1999-2000, and a visiting scholar at the Center for Latin American Studies at the University of California at Berkeley in 2000-2001. He retired early in 2011 from Providence College with the rank of professor emeritus. His writing and editing credits include numerous books and also a number of websites. A noted authority in Latin America, and especially the Catholic Church in Latin America, he contributed to films on Latin America and wrote numerous articles, chapters, and book reviews for scholarly and theological publications.

He died quietly on November 21, 2011 at the Priory of St. Thomas Aquinas at Providence College. The Mass of Christian burial was celebrated on November 28, 2011. Fr. David Orique, O.P., (Western Province) preached and Fr. Louis Morrone, O.P., Socius, presided. He was laid to rest with his fellow Dominican Friars in All Saints Cemetery in Des Plaines, Illinois.

KEVIN DAVID O'ROURKE, O.P.

Fr. O'Rourke was born on March 3, 1927 in Park Ridge, IL. His parents were William Joseph O'Rourke and Winifred Ann Stanton O'Rourke. Fr. O'Rourke was the youngest in the family. He had seven siblings who all preceded him in death: Winifred, Mary, Sr. Mary Winfrida, R.S.M., William, Agnes, Kathleen and Rita.

Fr. O'Rourke was regarded as a leading authority on health care ethics and bioethics, writing several books and publishing over a hundred articles examining such issues as genetic testing, surrogate decision-making and physician-assisted suicide. For many years he wrote a column, "Ethical Issues," published in the quarterly publication of St. Louis University Medical Center in St. Louis, Missouri. His best-known book is *Health Care Ethics: A Theological Analysis*, written with Fr. Benedict Ashley, O.P., and now in its 5th edition.

A 1945 graduate of Fenwick High School in Oak Park, IL, he attended the University of Notre Dame for two years before entering the Dominican Order in 1947. He made his first profession on September 15, 1948 and was ordained to the priesthood on May 27, 1954 and received his JCD in 1958.

After teaching canon law and serving as President of Aquinas Institute of Theology, he accepted a post-doctoral fellowship at the University of Chicago. When the Catholic Hospital Association (CHA) realized a need to respond to a growing number of inquiries in regard to the ethics of abortion and other ethical issues in health care, they hired Fr. O'Rourke, who eventually became director of Medico-Moral Affairs at CHA.

Fr. O'Rourke was also a Member of the National Advisory Committee for the U.S. Bishops and Consultant to their Committee on Canon Law; Chairman of the Religious Life Committee and of the Committee to Evaluate the Revised Code of Canon Law of the Canon Law Society of America.

He founded and served as Director of the Center for Health Care Ethics at St. Louis from 1979-1999. During this time he was consulted in several high profile cases, including that of Nancy Cruzan (1990), a case that made its way to the United States Supreme Court. This landmark case helped clarify the diagnosis of "persistent vegetative state" and established the legal right of patients to refuse all medical treatments including artificial nutrition and hydration.

O'Rourke was a tireless researcher and writer. He excelled in applying classic moral concepts such as the principle of cooperation and the distinction between ordinary and extraordinary care. He held that patients could invoke this traditional distinction to reject even respiration and artificial nutrition and hydration on the basis of a calculation of burdens and benefits relative to the patient's ability to "pursue the purpose of life." This led to criticism by some who felt that his views were in conflict with Church teaching on the dignity of life.

At the time of his death, Fr. O'Rourke was a scholar at the Neiswanger Institute for Bioethics and Health Policy at Loyola University Medical Center in Chicago. It would not be an exaggeration to say that he was one of the major voices in Catholic health care ethics in the United States in the 20th century.

Fr. O'Rourke passed away peacefully at Rush Hospital in Chicago on March 28, 2012 at the age of 85. Earlier in the day at the hospital, he was telling everyone present in his room that he was "going home" that day. Funeral Mass and wake were held at St. Vincent Ferrer Church in River Forest, Illinois. Interment was at All Saints Cemetery in Des Plaines, Illinois.

JOHN THOMAS ROBERT DOLEHIDE, O.P.

John Thomas Dolehide, the first of four children of John Thomas Dolehide, Sr. and Marie Veronica Benner, was born in Chicago, Illinois on September 4, 1918. As a child he attended St. Anselm primary school, followed by St. Dorothy, both in Chicago. He spent his first year of high school at St. Theresa in Decatur and then finished the remaining years of high school at De La Salle in Chicago, graduating in 1936. For the next four years he studied at De Paul University, where he majored in classical languages.

All of his initial formation was conducted at St. Thomas Aquinas Priory in River Forest, Illinois. On the Feast of St. Dominic, August 4, 1940, he received the habit and the religious name, Robert. After completing the Novitiate, he made his first profession of religious vows on August 5, 1941. He was assigned to philosophical study and subsequently earned a Bachelors Degree in Philosophy in 1944. On August 5th of the same year he made his Solemn Profession. Proceeding to the study of Theology, he continued his academic training at the Dominican House of Studies for the next four years. During this time he received the various Orders leading up to the Priesthood, and he was ordained on June 5, 1947.

Fr. Dolehide's first assignment was to work with the Preacher's Institute at St. Pius in Chicago, after which he became assistant pastor at St. Dominic Parish in New Orleans, Louisiana. He then returned to the Chicago area to teach for a year at Fenwick High School, our Dominican high school in Oak Park, Illinois. He then journeyed South again, where at Rosaryville in Ponchatoula, Louisiana, he served as chaplain and teacher from 1951-57. For the next two years he served as chaplain of St. Michael's College in Santa Fe, New Mexico, during which time he was also superior of the community. From 1959-66 he was assistant pastor at Holy Rosary Parish in Minneapolis, Minnesota and afterwards he served in the same capacity at St. Dominic's in Denver, Colorado for two years, Holy Rosary in Houston, Texas for three years, and one year at Nativity Parish in Campti, Louisiana.

After these first 20 years of priestly ministry, the Province sent Fr. Dolehide to study Theology for two years at Marquette University in Milwaukee, Wisconsin where he wrote a Master's Thesis entitled, "Orders as a Sacrament." This enabled him to teach at Aquinas Junior College in Nashville, Tennessee, where he also served as chaplain for ten years beginning in 1974. In 1984 he became Director of the Dominican Laity, and in 1985 he was assigned as associate pastor of St. Patrick Church in McHenry, Illinois. He was transferred to St. Peter's in Geneva, Illinois in 1988 and then to St. Catharine of Alexandria in Oak Lawn, Illinois in 1991, serving his longest stint as associate pastor there until 2006.

Having ministered as a Dominican Priest for 60 years, Fr. Dolehide moved to the assisted living center at St. Pius V Priory in Chicago in 2006 and then to Resurrection Life Nursing Center in 2010. On the night of July 26, 2012, he was having difficulty breathing and was taken to the emergency room. Having suffered from congestive heart failure the previous few years, his heart was worn out. He received Viaticum and the Apostolic Pardon from his Prior, Fr. Michael Kyte, and went home to the Lord on July 27, 2012. Funeral Mass and wake were held at St. Vincent Church in River Forest, Illinois and he was buried at All Saints Cemetery in Des Plaines, Illinois.

BENEDICT GARY BAER, O.P.

Gary Baer was born on January 3, 1946 in Chicago to Francis Baer and Juanita Bushnell, both of whom are deceased. He attended St. Patrick's Grade School in St. Charles, Illinois, and St. Edward's Central Catholic High School in Elgin, Illinois, graduating in 1964.

He received the Dominican Habit as a Cooperator Brother on December 19, 1965 at St. Rose Priory in Dubuque Iowa (he was the last brother in the province to receive the traditional black scapular habit of the brothers, and said he was always proud of it). He was given the religious name of Benedict. He made his first profession a year later on December 20, 1966. In Dubuque, he taught 4th grade religion and served as refectorian, assistant sacristan, and in the tailor shop from 1965 until 1969, when he was assigned to St. Albert the Great Priory in Minneapolis. Although he originally went there to pursue studies in religious education, he accepted a position as Director of Religious Education at the parish. He helped establish a pre-school at St. Albert's and served as a representative to the parish Council.

He remained at St. Albert's until 1978, with the exception of one year when he worked in the Registrar's office at the Angelicum in Rome. He brought all of his insight and organizational skills to that job, but found the work frustrating and only remained a year. In his straightforward manner, he told the provincial at the time that the Angelicum's systems were about "three centuries behind the times."

In 1978, he accepted a position as Youth Director in a parish in St. Paul, and he remained there until 1982. He served in a similar capacity at St. Vincent Ferrer in River Forest, Illinois. He went to Aquinas College in Grand Rapids in 1985, where he completed a bachelor's degree in religious education and also served as Director of Student Activities.

In 1994, he moved on to teach at Greater Muskegon (Michigan) Catholic School. He loved high school work, and made significant contributions to the spiritual life of the student body. When he left Muskegon in 2002, he spent several years working in the Vocations Office, and his last full-time assignment was to St. Paul Catholic Center at Indiana University. During that time he was involved in interreligious dialogue, especially with the Buddhist community.

These diverse assignments showed his many gifts, both administrative and pastoral, and demonstrated his love of the Order, of his brothers, and of those to whom he ministered. He made a deep impression upon people wherever he was assigned.

In 2010, his health had declined significantly; he had progressively lost most of his eye sight due to diabetes, and suffered from chronic obstructive pulmonary disease. His health continued to deteriorate, and he began dialysis in September of 2011. Despite his health challenges, he never lost his zest for life, his desire to be, as he said, "out and about," and his love for his companion dogs, Angus and Murphy.

He went home to he Lord on August 26, 2012 while visiting friends in the Chicago area. Mass of Christian Burial and Office of the Dead was celebrated at St. Vincent Ferrer Parish in River Forest, Illinois. He was buried at All Saints Cemetery in Des Plaines, Illinois.

JOSEPH PETER KENNY, O.P

Father Joseph Peter Kenny, O.P., 77, a native of Chicago, Illinois, was born on January 12, 1936. He made his first profession as a Dominican Friar on August 31, 1957 and was ordained to the priesthood on April 15, 1963. Fr. Kenny was a missionary in Africa for nearly 50 years. He left for Nigeria at the request of the Holy See as resource person knowledgeable in Arabic and Islam, since there was a need at the very least to secure understanding and peace between the country's large Christian and Muslim communities.

Father Joe took time to learn Arabic in Rome, Tunisia, and Cairo, and to obtain a Ph.D. in Arabic and Islamic studies at the University of Edinburgh, UK. After working in northern Nigeria, he taught subjects on Islamic philosophy and theology for 22 years at the government-owned University of Ibadan, where he served as Chairman of the Department of Religious Studies. He also helped develop the Dominican Institute in Ibadan, where he taught courses on philo-sophy, theology, and communications for hundreds of lay students and seminarians, many of whom are now missionary priests in the United States.

He was fluent in 13 languages and recently travelled to both Iran and Lebanon in the interest of inter-faith dialogue. A citizen of Nigeria as well as the United States, he was a consultant to the Association of Episcopal Conferences of West Africa, the Catholic Bishops Conference of Nigeria (CBCN) Commission for Inter-Religious Dialogue, and the Nigerian Field Society. He wrote over 230 articles and books, with particular emphasis on Christian-

Muslim relations. These, together with the largest collection of the works of St. Thomas Aquinas, are on his website: www.josephkenny.joyeurs.com.

Fr. Kenney died of cancer on January 28, 2013 in Washington DC. He was survived by his brothers Henry and Paul, and sisters Catherine and Margaret, as well as his fellow Nigerian Dominican priests and laity, and all who are brothers and sisters in Christ. A funeral Mass was celebrated at the Dominican House of Studies, 487 Michigan Ave., N.E., Washington D.C. on Saturday, February 2, 2013 at 11:00 AM.

BENEDICT M. WINSTON ASHLEY, O.P.

Winston Norman Ashley was born to Arthur Burton Ashley and Bertha Moore on May 3, 1915 in Neodesha, Kansas. His oldest and only sibling, Richard, had been born six years earlier. While both were still young, the family moved to Blackwell, Oklahoma, where Winston received his primary and secondary education in the public schools there from 1921-33.

Upon graduating from high school, Winston began his under-graduate studies at the University of Chicago. In 1937, he received an M.A. from the same school in the field of Comparative Literature. It was during the following year that he received a unique grace (which he attributed to the intercession of the Blessed Virgin) in which the spear wound from Christ's side made a powerful impression upon his consciousness, leading him eventually to enter the Catholic Church. His parents had been Protestant, and he himself had in recent years been a committed atheist and communist. The study of St. Thomas, to whom he had been introduced by Mortimer Adler at U. of C., had paved the way for his intellectual acquiescence to the Faith, and he would later devote much of his academic work as a Dominican to expounding the thought of the same Angelic Doctor.

After being received into the Church in 1938 and taking the Baptismal name Joseph, the new convert moved the following year to South Bend, Indiana, where he received his first PhD in 1941 in Political Philosophy. On the Feast of St. Dominic in 1941, he received the Dominican habit in River Forest, IL; four years and one day later, he made Solemn Profession *usque ad mortem* at the Dominican Camp in Menominee, Michigan. On June 4th, 1948, the Feast of Our Lady, Queen of Apostles, Fr. Benedict Mary Ashley was ordained to the Priesthood of Jesus Christ. Having spent the decade in studies in River Forest, he received a Lectorate in Theology in 1949, followed by a second doctorate in Philosophy from the Pontifical Faculty there.

Fr. Ashley then began his impressively prolific and distinguished career in the Order's intellectual apostolate as a professor, author, lecturer and consultant. An exhaustive list would be overwhelming, but highlights include: A little under two decades (1951-69) as Instructor/Professor of Philosophy at Aquinas Institute, during which time he contributed greatly to expounding the famous 'River Forest School' of Thomism through his work for the Albertus Magnus Lyceum; during this time he served 5 years (1958-63) as Director of the aforementioned Lyceum and 7 years (1962-69) as both Regent of Studies for the Province and President of Aquinas Institute; for the next 3 years he was Professor of Social Philosophy & Theology at the Institute of Religion & Human Development in Houston, TX (1969-72); he then served as Professor of Moral Theology at Aquinas Institute from 1972 until he assumed Emeritus status in 1980; both before and after assuming Emeritus status, he was frequently appointed Visiting Professor at a number of fine institutions, including the University of Chicago, the Pontifical John Paul II Institute for Studies on Marriage & Family—to which his contribution was considerable, St. Xavier College, St. Mary's Dominican College, St. Mary of the Lake Seminary, Catholic University of America, St. Mary's Seminary, and others.

Fr. Ashley likewise served in numerous consulting positions: He was for some years in the post-Vatican II period a consultant in moral theology for the Committee on Doctrine and Pastoral Practice of the U.S. Conference of Catholic Bishops, and he helped to develop their 3rd edition of the Ethical and Religious Directives for Catholic Health Care Facilities; he was a Theological Consultant for the Mercy Health Care Corporation, a member of the Theological Advisory Council of the Danforth Foundation and Senior Fellow of the Pope John XXIII Center for Medical Ethics Research & Education, to name only a few. He was also the first President of the Midwestern Association of Theological Schools and a founding member of the Board of the Association of Chicago Theological Schools.

Fr. Ashley's output in the written apostolate was likewise immense. Just a few of his many well-known books include *Health Care Ethics: A Catholic Theological Analysis (currently in its 5th ed.), The Arts of Learning & Communication, Theologies of the Body: Humanist & Christian, The Dominicans, Living the Truth in Love: A Biblical Introduction to Moral Theology, Choosing a Worldview & Value System: An Ecumenical Apologetics, The Ashley Reader: Redeeming Reason,* and *The Way Toward Wisdom: An Interdisciplinary & Contextual Introduction to Metaphysics,* among many other books, not to mention countless articles in journals, anthologies, etc. His autobiography, *Barefoot Journeying*, has recently been published by New Priory Press.

Two of Fr. Benedict's most prestigious awards and honors are the *Pro Ecclesia et Pontifice* Medal conferred by John Paul II and the post-doctoral Master in Sacred Theology from the University of St. Thomas Aquinas in Rome.

Even into his 90's, Fr. Ashley would periodically teach formal theology courses at Aquinas Institute. Just as he had taught and formed young Dominicans during his first years of formal ministry, likewise toward the end of his life he again lived for many years in the studentate community (this time in St. Louis), where his edifying example of Dominican life continued to inspire many young brothers in initial formation.

Due to declining health, Fr. Ashley moved to St. Pius V Priory in Chicago in 2009, and in 2013 at the age of 97 he was still earnestly engaged in the 'apostolate of the pen.' Never content merely to shine, Fr. Ashley studiously sought to illumine others even into his final days. After a few short weeks of weakness and confusion, he slipped into a coma and died a few days later on February 23, 2013. Funeral Mass and Office of the Dead was celebrated at St. Vincent Ferrer Church and he was buried at All Saints Cemetery in Des Plaines, Illinois.

RODERICK MARVIN BROWN, O.P.

Roderick Marvin Brown was born in Chicago, Illinois on June 17, 1942, the youngest of five children, to William Brown and Isabel Gordon. He attended Holy Angels Grammar School, Quigley Preparatory High School, and graduated from Corpus Christi High School in 1960.

Father Brown served in the U.S. Navy as a corpsman from 1960 to 1964. He graduated with a B.A. in Liberal Arts from Chicago State University in 1974. He entered the Dominican Novitiate in 1974 and made his first profession of vows on October 4, 1975 at St. Rose of Lima Priory in Dubuque, Iowa. He continued his studies for the priesthood at the Aquinas Institute of Theology and was ordained on August 8, 1979 in Dubuque, Iowa. Father Brown continued advanced studies at the doctorate level at LaSalle University in Philadelphia, PA in Theocentric Counseling.

In 1979, Father Brown was assigned to campus ministry at Texas Southern University (Houston, TX), where he served four years until becoming Vicar for Black Ministry in the Genesee Region of the Diocese of Lansing, MI and pastor for Christ the King Parish in Flint, MI.

Later he was part of the Team Ministry at Visitation Parish in Chicago. He was invited to Buffalo, New York, where he spent 14 years as vicar to the Central Buffalo Vicariate, serving St. Matthew and St. Bartholomew Parish, and was the founding pastor of St. Martin de Porres Parish. There, he embraced the opportunity to serve a large population of African American Catholics struggling with poverty.

Though Fr. Brown came to consider Buffalo "home", he returned to St. Pius V Priory in Chicago in 2002 on limited service due to his diagnosis with Multiple Sclerosis. In 2008, he moved to Resurrection Life Center in Chicago. He died on the morning of October 16, 2013 while recovering from surgery at Resurrection Hospital. The Office of the Dead and a Mass of Christian Burial were celebrated at St. Vincent Ferrer Parish in River Forest, Illinois on Thursday, October 24, 2013. He was buried at All Saints Cemetery in Des Plaines, Illinois.

JEROME MATTHIAS WALSH, O.P.

Jerome Matthias Walsh was born on April 10, 1932, to Leonard and Margaret Walsh in Durand, Illinois, 100 miles northwest of Chicago. After two years at Loras College in Dubuque, Iowa, he made his first profession in the Dominican Order on August 31, 1952, receiving the religious name of Matthias. He attended the College of St. Thomas Aquinas in River Forest, Illinois from 1952-55, receiving a B.A. in philosophy. After three years of theological studies at the Studium of St. Rose of Lima in Dubuque, Iowas, he was ordained to the priesthood on May 24, 1958.

From 1959-76, Fr. Walsh worked in various Dominican ministries in Nigeria, West Africa. He was Vicar General of the Diocese of Sokoto, Nigeria, and pastor for parishes including St. Vincent Ferrer in Malumfashi and Our Lady of Fatima in Gusau. In the 1970s he was Lecturer at the Dominican Seminary of Sts.

Peter & Paul in Ibadan, Nigeria. He was instrumental in the early years of the Dominican province now existing in Nigeria, serving as Vocation Director and Novice Master.

When he returned to the United States in 1976, Fr. Walsh preached parish missions for several years in the Midwest and worked in campus ministry. He then returned overseas, working for several years in Papua New Guinea in ministries sponsored by the Australian Dominican Province. In his concluding years of service, he was Vocation Director and Novice Master for his Province as well as the Director of the Dominican Shrine of St. Jude Thaddeus and Vicar for Mission Advancement.

Fr. Walsh was assigned in 2005 to limited service, residing at Blessed Sacrament Priory in Madison, Wisconsin, where he lived for eight years before he was diagnosed with pancreatic cancer. Fr. Walsh died on November 3, 2013 after several months in hospice care in Madison.

Fr. Walsh is survived by his brother Jim and sister-in-law Barb Walsh, of Beloit, Wisconsin, as well as numerous nieces, nephews, and cousins.

The Mass of Christian Burial was held at Blessed Sacrament Church on November 7, 2013. He was buried in Madison, Wisconsin at Resurrection Cemetery in the Dominican plot.

JOHN HAROLD GERLACH, O.P.

John Gerlach was born (Harold William Gerlach) on February 2, 1937, to Harold and Anna (Low) Gerlach in Sioux City, Iowa, where he attended St. Boniface parochial school. He graduated from Heelan High School in 1954, then studied for two years at Loras College in Dubuque, Iowa before entering the Dominicans, Province of St. Albert the Great and given the religious name, John Baptist. He made his first profession in the Dominican Order on August 31, 1957 at St. Peter Martyr Priory in Winona, Minnesota. Father Gerlach continued studies at the Dominican House of Studies in River Forest, Illinois and Aquinas Institute at St. Rose of Lima Priory in Dubuque, Iowa before he was ordained to the priesthood there on April 15, 1963.

In his first Dominican ministry, Fr. Gerlach was assigned to the faculty at Fenwick High School in Oak Park, Illinois in 1964. For almost 30 years, he served as Chaplain for the Dominican Sisters, from 1967-69, 1980-83, and from 2001-13 in Sinsinawa, Wisconsin and from 1990-2001 in Springfield, Illinois. He also served the Dominican Province of St. Albert the Great as Vicar Provincial from 1985-1990 and as Novice Master from 1969-74. In the 1970s, Fr. Gerlach led campus ministry at South Dakota State University, worked in preaching ministry in Oak Park, Illinois and was associate pastor at Blessed Sacrament Parish in Madison, Wisconsin.

On November 21, 2013, Fr. Gerlach died at Mercy Hospital in Dubuque, Iowa after suffering a heart attack earlier in the week. A Mass of Christian Burial and wake was held at Queen of the Rosary Chapel, Dominican Motherhouse in Sinsinawa, Wisconsin on November 26 & 27, 2013. Office of the Dead and a Mass of Christian Burial was also held in at St. Vincent Ferrer Parish in River Forest, Illinois on December 2, 2013. Burial was at All Saints Cemetery in Des Plaines, Illinois. Fr. Gerlach was survived by his brother Howard (Carole) Gerlach, and sisters, Estelle Gerlach, and Jean (Daniel) Raih and their immediate and extended families.

MICHAEL GERARD KYTE, O.P.

Michael Gerard Kyte was born on April 20, 1953 in Sydney, Nova Scotia, Canada to Arthur Stanislaus and Marie Elizabeth (Gillis) Kyte. Michael had four brothers and three sisters. Fr. Kyte was baptized on May 3, 1953 at Sacred Heart Parish in Sydney, Nova Scotia. He attended St John's Academy in New Glasgow,

Nova Scotia from 1958-64. The family moved back to Sydney and he continued school at St. Joseph Academy then on to Sheriff Junior High School. He graduated high school from Sydney Academy in 1971. In the Fall of 1971 he began university studies at Dalhousie University in Halifax, Nova Scotia, spent a year studying French abroad at Universite de Nice, Nice, France, then graduated with a Bachelor of Art Degree in Political Science in 1975.

The year Fr. Kyte graduated from the university, he worked as a Rehabilitation Worker for The Canadian Rehabilitation Council for the Disabled (CRCD) and continued there for three years. Expanding his horizons beyond Canada, he joined the Canadian University Service Overseas (CUSO) and worked as an English teacher in Nigeria, West Africa from 1978-80, the place where he first met the Dominican Friars. He then returned to Canada and taught school for the Government of the Northwest Territories for one year.

Fr. Kyte entered the novitiate for the Province of St. Albert the Great, having been influenced by the friars from our province working at our mission in Nigeria. He was received on August 16, 1981 and professed his first vows on August 22, 1982 at St. Dominic Priory in Denver, Colorado. From 1982-87 he studied at Aquinas Institute of Theology in St. Louis, Missouri. He was ordained a deacon on May 10, 1986 at the Basilica of St. Louis the King of France in St. Louis. He did a deaconate internship from July to December of 1986 at Visitation Parish in Chicago, Illinois. He was ordained to the priesthood on May 24, 1987 at St. Vincent Ferrer Parish in River Forest, Illinois.

His first assignment was to the Catholic Community in Englewood in the South side of Chicago through St. Basil Parish. After six years he was called to internal ministry for the province and from 1993-2003 he served as novice master at St. Dominic Priory in Denver, Colorado. During these years, he was on the founding board of the Colorado Dominican Vocation Foundation, to raise funds for the novitiate program. After ten years as novice master he was granted a one- year sabbatical study program. In 2004 he was appointed as parochial vicar at St. Vincent Ferrer Parish in River Forest, Illinois and served the parish well for over nine years and the Dominican Community there for six years as prior.

In December 2012 he was diagnosed with end stage colon cancer while at a provincial council meeting in Albuquerque, New Mexico. For the next fifteen months his life was consumed with cancer treatment. Throughout his illness he continued to minister and was beloved by many.

He was under hospice care for only one day before he died peacefully on March 27, 2014 at home at St. Pius Priory surrounded by his Dominican brothers, his brother Lorne and a few friends.

On Monday, March 31, 2014, at St. Vincent Ferrer Church, Evening Prayer Office of the Dead was sung at 4:00 p.m. followed by a visitation where hundreds came to pray and say goodbye. On Tuesday, April 1, 2014 the Mass of the Resurrection was celebrated. Fr. Charles Bouchard, O.P., Prior Provincial, presided and Fr. Louis Morrone, O.P., preached. All seven of his siblings from Canada attended, as did most of his nieces and nephews. He was buried at All Saints Cemetery in Des Plaines, Illinois in the Dominican section.

THOMAS AQUINAS MORRISON, O.P.

Thomas Lawrence Morrison was born on July 1, 1928 in Chicago, Illinois to Thomas Lawrence and Virginia Agnes (Nangle) Morrison. The second of three children, he was baptized at St. Justin Martyr Church on July 15, 1928 and confirmed on May 25, 1939 at St. Philip Neri Church in Chicago. From 1934-42 he attended St. Philip Neri Grammar School and 1942-44, Archbishop

Quigley Preparatory Seminary, both in Chicago. He then attended Loras Academy from 1944-45 and then studied History & Political Science at Loras College in Dubuque, Iowa.

Fr. Morrison entered the Order of Preachers on June 24, 1948 at St. Thomas Aquinas Priory in River Forest, Illinois and was given the religious name, Thomas Aquinas. He professed simple vows on June 25, 1949 and solemn vows on June 25, 1952 at St. Thomas Aquinas Priory in River Forest where he continued his studies in Philosophy. From 1952-56 he studied Theology at St. Rose Priory in Dubuque, Iowa. He was ordained to the diaconate in October 1952 and to the priesthood on May 19, 1955, both at St. Rose Priory. In 1960 he earned Master of Arts in Theology from Xavier Institute of Theology in Chicago, Illinois.

Fr. Morrison taught Philosophy and Theology from 1956-68 at DePaul University, Xavier Institute of Theology and Loyola University in Chicago, University of Albuquerque, Dominican College in Racine, Wisconsin, and the University of Dallas in Irving, Texas. His parish pastoral ministry from 1968-72 included serving as associate pastor of St. Vincent Ferrer Church in River Forest, Illinois. For many years before his death he worked as a chaplain in several hospitals with his longest assignment at Holy Cross Hospital in Chicago from 1985-2002.

In 2002 he was placed on limited service with residence at St. Pius V Priory in Chicago. His health slowly deteriorated and he was transferred in 2010 to Resurrection Life Nursing Center in Chicago. His few years at Resurrection Life Center were pleasant as he lived with dementia. He died peacefully there on April 1, 2014. Office of the Dead and the Mass of Christian Burial was held at St. Vincent Ferrer Church in River Forest, Illinois on April 8, 2014. He was buried at All Saints Cemetery in Des Plaines, Illinois.

GILBERT LEROY HENSLEY, O.P.

Gilbert Leroy Hensley was born in Milwaukee, Wisconsin on January 18, 1941, the youngest of three boys, to Charles L. and Lillian E. (Scheefe) Hensley. Both his parents died by the time he was nine years old. He was raised by his foster parents, Mr. & Mrs. John Schmeling. He attended Cass Street School and St. John Cathedral Grade School and High School in Milwaukee, Wisconsin before moving to Nashville, Tennessee, where he graduated from Father Ryan High School on June 2,1960.

Br. Hensley entered the Order as a Cooperator Brother on March 19, 1961 at St. Thomas Aquinas Priory in River Forest, Illinois. He was given the religious name Angelus and made his simple profession of vows on March 20, 1962 and solemn profession on March 20, 1968 both at St. Thomas Aquinas Priory.

Most of his religious life, as a brother, was spent working in the priories and parishes of the province. From 1962-1971 he remained at St. Thomas Aquinas Priory doing domestic work in the priory. From 1971-1986 he assisted at St. Vincent Ferrer Parish as sacristan and helped in the grammar school. In 1986 he moved to Madison, Wisconsin and was part of the support staff at Edgewood Elementary School and lived at Blessed Sacrament Priory where he was the house bursar for several years. He remained in Madison until 2005 at which time he relocated to the Motherhouse of the Dominican Sisters of the Most Holy Rosary in Sinsinawa, Wisconsin. There he helped with many tasks of the motherhouse from helping with the older sisters, to assisting in the maintenance department, to decorating the house for holidays. He was a beloved brother to the sisters and the staff of the motherhouse.

In May 2014 Br. Gilbert had emergency abdominal surgery at Mercy Hospital in Dubuque, Iowa, suffering major post-operative compli-cations with anesthesia, infection and kidney function. After a second surgery he was unable to regain his strength. He continued to decline and died on May 31, 2014 at the hospital. He was 73 years old.

Funeral services were held on Wednesday, June 4, 2014, at Holy Rosary Chapel, Dominican Motherhouse, Sinsinawa, Wisconsin. His body was received at the motherhouse at 9:30 a.m. followed by morning prayer and sharing of memories led by Sister Mary Ellen Winston, O.P. Mass of Christian Burial followed at 10:30 a.m. with Fr. Louis Morrone, O.P, Socius, presiding and Fr. Jack Risley, O.P., preaching. Fr. Steven Kuhlmann, O.P. presided over the graveside service and burial, which was at Resurrection Cemetery, Dominican Friars Section in Madison, Wisconsin.

WILFRED GABRIEL HOFF, O.P.

Wilfred Francis Hoff was born on August 23, 1918 in Denver, Colorado to John Francis and Rose (Spitzmiller) Hoff. His father died when he was very young and his mother remarried Joseph Nachbauer. Fr. Hoff has one half sister, Lorraine (Nachbauer) Williams, of Burbank, California who has six children. Fr. Hoff was baptized on September 8, 1918 at St. Catherine of Siena Church in Denver. He attended grammar school at St. Dominic Elementary School from 1925-32, Lake Junior High from 1932-33, and North High School from 1933-1936. In 1936 his vocation led him to St. Thomas Seminary in Denver where he studied the next four years. He entered the Dominican Novitiate on August 4, 1940 and was given the religious name Gabriel. His first profession was August 5, 1941 and solemn profession August 5, 1944. He continued his studies for the priesthood and was ordained on June 5, 1947. All his formation and education was done at St. Thomas Aquinas Priory in River Forest, Illinois.

His first assignment was associate pastor at Blessed Sacrament Parish in Madison, Wisconsin from 1948-51. He served over the next thirty years at the following places: 1951-53 as associate pastor at Holy Name Parish in Kansas City, Missouri; 1953-61 as associate pastor and 1961-67 as pastor at St. Helena Parish in Amite, Louisiana; 1967-70 as hospital chaplain at Methodist Hospital and helped at Holy Rosary Parish in Houston, Texas; 1970-76 as associate pastor at St. Dominic Parish in Denver, Colorado; and 1976-83 as associate pastor at Holy Ghost Parish in Hammond, Louisiana. In 1983 he moved to Albuquerque, New Mexico and worked in the Diocese of Santa Fe for the next 25 years and lived at the Newman Center with the Dominican Community there.

He moved to Chicago, Illinois to St. Pius V Priory, assisted living center, in 2008. As his health deteriorated, he was moved in 2010 to Holy Family of Nazareth Nursing Facility for a short time then to Resurrection Life Center in Chicago, where he spent the rest of days. His hearing became progressively worse over the years and though he couldn't always hear you, he was always pleased to have visitors and only wished one thing, that God would bring him home to his eternal reward.

On July 18, 2014 Fr. Hoff died peacefully at Resurrection Hospital. At the time of his death he was 95 years old and the oldest member of the province. Office of the Dead and Mass of Christian Burial was held at St. Vincent Ferrer Church in River Forest, Illinois on July 24, 2014. Fr. Charles Bouchard, O.P., Prior Provincial, presided and Fr. George Reynolds, O.P., preached. His family was represented at the funeral by one niece and one nephew from California. Because of age and health, his sister, Lorraine, was unable to attend. He was buried at All Saints Cemetery in Des Plaines, Illinois in the Dominican section.

BEDE ROBERT JAGOE, O.P.

Bede Robert Jagoe was born (Robert Joseph Jagoe) on January 24, 1934 in St. Paul, Minnesota. His parents were Francis Charles Jagoe and Marie Catherine (Kokes) Jagoe. He had one sister, Mary Frances (John) Modjeski, and one brother, Patrick Henry

(Elizabeth) Jagoe. Fr. Jagoe attended Hill School and St. Luke's Grammar School in St. Paul, Minnesota and St. Patrick's Grammar School in Mauston, Wisconsin from 1939-47. He graduated from Mauston Public High School in 1951. He then studied at Loras College in Dubuque, Iowa from 1951-53 with the intent to join the Order. He received the Dominican habit on August 30, 1953 and received the religious name, Bede. He professed his first vows on August 31, 1954 at St. Peter Martyr Priory in Winona, Minnesota and final vows on August 31, 1957 at St. Thomas Aquinas Priory in River Forest, Illinois. Fr. Jagoe continued his studies at the Dominican House of Studies in River Forest, Illinois then later at Aquinas Institute of Theology at St. Rose Priory in Dubuque, Iowa where he was ordained to the priesthood on June 4, 1960.

Fr. Jagoe was sent to the foreign missions for his first ministry. He worked in Nigeria in West Africa from 1961-84. Fr. Jagoe was involved in pastoral ministry in the following places: Our Lady of Fatima, Gusai; and St. Vincent Ferrer Parish, Malumfashi. He also lived in Ibadan where he was the prior of the community and held various positions in the diocese in Catechetics and the Liturgical Commission. When he retuned to the United States, he was involved in the following ministries: 1984-85 as Spiritual Director, Notre Dame Institute for Clergy Education, Notre Dame, Indiana; 1985-86 as chaplain at the Dominican Sister's Motherhouse, Sinsinawa, Wisconsin; 1986-87 as Acting Director, Center for Continuing Formation in Ministry, University of Notre Dame; 1987-89 & 1994-97 Director, St. Dominic Mission Society, Chicago, Illinois; 1991-93 Director of Campus Ministry, St. Louis University, St. Louis, Missouri; 1997-2003 Director, Shrine of St. Jude Thaddeus, Chicago, Illinois. His last ministry from 2003-10 was as part-time chaplain at Midway Airport, Chicago, Illinois.

As his health declined he was on limited service at St. Pius V Priory in Chicago, Illinois and was eventually admitted to Resurrection Life Center where he lived until his death. He was in and out of the hospital several times in the last year of his life. He died on August 5, 2014 at Resurrection Hospital. He was eighty years old. Office of the Dead and Mass of Christian Burial was celebrated. Fr. Jagoe's classmate, Fr. Benjamin Russell, preached the Mass at St. Vincent Ferrer Parish in River Forest, Illinois on August 9, 2014. Burial was held at All Saints Cemetery in Des Plaines, Illinois.

BENJAMIN JOSEPH RUSSELL, O.P.

Fr. Benjamin J. Russell was born (Joseph Francis Russell) on July 24, 1933, to Joseph Allen Russell and Margaret Catherine (Dunleavy) Russell in Boston, Massachusetts. He had one brother, Thomas Edward Russell. Fr. Russell attended St. Francis de Sales Grammar School in Charlestown, Massachusetts from 1938-47 and Boston College High School graduating in 1951. He then studied at Loras College in Dubuque, Iowa from 1951-53 with the intent to join the Order. He received the Dominican habit on August 30, 1953 and received the religious name, Benjamin. He professed his first vows on August 31, 1954 at St. Peter Martyr Priory in Winona, Minnesota and final vows on August 31, 1957 at St. Thomas Aquinas Priory in River Forest, Illinois. Fr. Russell continued his studies at the Dominican House of Studies in River Forest, Illinois then later at Aquinas Institute of Theology at St. Rose Priory in Dubuque, Iowa where he was ordained to the priesthood on June 4, 1960.

Fenwick High School in Oak Park, Illinois was his first ministry assignment where he taught Theology and English from 1961-64. In advanced studies he earned an MA in English Literature and Ph.D. in Philosophy from Loyola University, Chicago, Illinois. Fr. Russell served on the faculty of Aquinas Institute from 1964-70 and was Master of students during some of these years. He was then assigned to pastoral ministry as the pastor of Blessed Sacrament Parish in Madison, Wisconsin from 1971-77. He then joined the faculty of Religious Studies at Edgewood College in Madison from 1977-85. He returned to teach at Aquinas Institute and served as the Academic Dean from 1985-90. From 1990-96 he returned to pastoral ministry and was pastor at St. Vincent Ferrer Parish in River Forest, Illinois. Fr. Russell then worked in the Office of Mission of Advancement for the province from 1997-2001. For the following five years he was on limited service, living in Madison, Wisconsin, St. Louis, Missouri and eventually, St. Pius V Priory in Chicago. In 2011 he was asked to join the community at St. Thomas Aquinas Catholic Center at Purdue University in West Lafayette, Indiana, which was where he was living at the time of his death.

Fr. Russell came to Chicago to preach the funeral of his classmate, Fr. Bede Jagoe, on August 9, 2014 in Chicago. He was to return home to West Lafayette, Indiana on August 11, 2014. Early that morning he collapsed and suffered a severe heart attack. He was taken to the hospital where he died later that afternoon on August 11, 2014. He was eighty-one years old. Office of the Dead and Mass of Christian Burial was celebrated with Fr. James Marchionda preaching at St. Vincent Ferrer Parish in River Forest, Illinois on August 16, 2014. Burial was held at All Saints Cemetery in Des Plaines, Illinois.

ROBERT JEROME BOTTHOF, O.P.

Robert Jerome Botthof was born on October 27, 1928 in Chicago, Illinois. He attended grammar school and high school in the Chicago area before entering the Christian Brothers. After a short time with the Christian Brothers he left and continued his education and married Mary Elizabeth Nutt in 1957. They had two children, James and Mary Alice. Mary died in 1980. Before entering the Dominicans he served in the United States Marine Corps from 1953-55 and then taught high school at Niles Township East and West from 1955-72. He earned a Doctorate in Education from Indiana University in 1969. He was principal of Oak Park and River Forest High School, Oak Park, Illinois from 1972-82.

In 1982, Fr. Botthof entered the Dominican Novitiate in Denver, Colorado and professed his simple vows on August 21, 1983 at St. Dominic Priory in Denver, Colorado and his solemn vows on August 30, 1986 at the Basilica of St. Louis in St. Louis, Missouri. He completed his studies at Aquinas Institute of Theology in St. Louis, Missouri. He was ordained to the priesthood on May 24, 1987 at St. Vincent Ferrer Parish in River Forest, Illinois.

As a Dominican priest, he served as the President/Principal of Fenwick High School in Oak Park, Illinois from 1987-94. He was instrumental in facilitating Fenwick High School's becoming coeducational. He was parochial vicar and later, pastor of St. Vincent Ferrer Parish in River Forest from 1995-04 and parochial vicar at St. Domitilla Parish in Hillside, Illinois from 2004-08. His last ministry was as the Pastoral Director of the Dominican Shrine of St. Jude in Chicago until 2012. He then joined the community at St. Paul's Catholic Center at Indiana University in Bloomington, Indiana for two years on limited service. Because of declining health he returned to Chicago to St. Pius V Priory-assisted living center a short time before he died.

On the afternoon of October 15, 2014 he died peacefully in his room at St. Pius with some of the brothers and priory staff with him.

Services were held at St. Vincent Ferrer Church in River Forest, Illinois on Monday, October 20, 2014, beginning with the reception of the body and Office of the Dead at 4:00PM and visitation until 6:00PM. Mass of Christian Burial was celebrated on Tuesday, October 21, 2014 at 10:00AM preceded by Sung Morning Prayer. Fr. Charles Bouchard, O.P., Prior Provincial, presided and preached. At the family's request, he was buried at Oak Hill Cemetery, Taylorville, Illinois.

JOHN CHARLES FABIAN, O.P.

John Charles Fabian was born on February 11, 1932 in Mingo Junction, Ohio to Michael and Anna (Krizan) Fabian. He was the youngest of ten children. His older brother, Cyril Fabian, is a member of the province. He attended elementary school at St. Agnes in Mingo Junction, Ohio and graduated from Catholic Central High School in Steubenville, Ohio in 1950.

Fr. Fabian entered the Dominican Novitiate in August 1952 at St. Peter Martyr Priory in Winona, Minnesota and was given the religious name, Basil. He made his first profession August 31, 1953 and his solemn profession on August 31, 1956. He continued his studies for the priesthood at Aquinas Institute in Dubuque, Iowa and was ordained to the priesthood on May 23, 1959 at St. Rose Priory in Dubuque.

As a priest, he served from 1960-72 as a high school Theology and Latin teacher at Fenwick High School in Oak Park, Illinois and later at Bishop Lynch High School in Dallas, Texas. From 1972-84 he was an associate pastor in various parishes and Catholic campus ministry centers in the province.

In 1984 he was commissioned as lieutenant in the U.S. Navy and served as a Navy chaplain over twenty years. He lived and worked in California for many years. In 2009 he returned to Chicago on limited service. He had a difficult time adjusting to life back in Chicago and so he returned to California in 2014. He was living alone and died there on October 29, 2014.

Office of the Dead and a Memorial Mass was celebrated at St. Pius V Priory, Chicago, Illinois on Saturday, November 22, 2014. Fr. Nick Monco, O.P. preached and Fr. Louis Morrone, O.P., prior, presided. He was cremated in California and buried at All Saints Cemetery, Des Plaines, Illinois.

FRANCIS EDWARD NOUZA, O.P.

Francis Edward Nouza was born on August 16, 1929 in Chicago to Francis and Martha (Benson) Nouza. He attended St. Lucy's Grammar School and Austin High School, both in Chicago. He then attended college at DePaul University in Chicago and later at Loras College in Dubuque. Fr. Nouza entered the Dominican Novitiate in 1951 and was given the religious name, Marcolinus. He made his first profession of vows on August 31, 1952 at St. Peter Martyr Priory in Winona, Minnesota and his solemn profession on August 31, 1955 at St. Thomas Aquinas Priory, River Forest, Illinois. He continued his studies for the priesthood in River Forest, Illinois and Dubuque, Iowa. He was ordained to the priesthood on May 24, 1958 at St. Rose Priory in Dubuque.

Shortly after his ordination he was assigned to work in California where he spent many years. Fr. Nouza taught high school at St. Vincent Ferrer High School in Vallejo, California. He also served at the following schools: Sacramento State College Newman Center, St. Albert's College, Oakland, San Jose State University, Cabot College, and University of San Francisco. In addition, Fr. Nouza served as chaplain of the Police Officers' Research Association of California and was Executive Director of Problems in Ethics and Policing in California for many years. In 1971 He received an M.S. in Administration of Justice from San Jose State College. He published articles on the moral obligations of citizens toward problems in law enforcement.

Fr. Nouza went on limited service and remained in California for several years before returning to Chicago in 2012 and living at St. Pius V Priory-assisted living center. His health continued to deteriorate and he was transferred to Resurrection Life Center in 2014. He died peacefully at Resurrection Life Center on February 19, 2015.

Office of the dead and Mass of Christian Burial was celebrated at St. Vincent Ferrer Church in River Forest, Illinois on Monday,

March 2, 2015. He was buried at All Saints Cemetery in Des Plaines, Illinois.

www.ingramcontent.com/pod-product-compliance
Lightning Source LLC
Chambersburg PA
CBHW070645030426
42337CB00020B/4171